IN THE Kitchen WITH Mary & Martha

A Cookbook Featuring
Oodles of Inspiration, Recipes & Tips

BARBOUR
PUBLISHING

Cover art and interior illustrations by Margy Ronning
Cover and interior design by Greg Jackson/Jackson Design Co.

Published by Barbour Publishing, Inc., P.O. Box 719, Uhrichsville, Ohio 44683
www.barbourbooks.com

Our mission is to publish and distribute inspirational products offering exceptional value and biblical encouragement to the masses.

 Member of the
Evangelical Christian
Publishers Association

Printed in China
5 4 3 2 1

Dedication

To our family and friends. . .
You are a blessing. We're so thankful to have you in our lives.

And to the super staff at Dover Avenue School. . .
Thanks for sharing your delicious dishes with us!

Meet Mary & Martha. . .

Hi, folks! We're Mary & Martha. Pleased to meet you!

We plan on spending lots of time in your kitchen, so we thought you'd like to know a bit about us first. . . .

I'm Martha, and I have a kitchen fetish. It is where I spend most of my time. I love to experiment with food and the preparation process—and sample my work. But some things I make are just too pretty to eat, and I'm rather disappointed to see the creations that took me hours to prepare disappear into my family's eager mouths within minutes. So I've learned to make fantastic homemade recipes appealing to both the eye and the palate using timesaving tips I'll share with you. Stick with me, and you'll be able to conquer anything in the kitchen—even if you're culinarily challenged (ahem. . .like my friend Mary).

Thanks for that wonderful vote of confidence, Martha. . . .

I'm Mary. I always say that the kitchen is the heart of the house. Where else can you find such warmth, family togetherness, and inspiration in one room? While I love to cook up tasty treats and meals for my family, I've always been the laid-back type who looks for ways to cut down on my kitchen time to make more family time. So I find my true inspiration in the easy, simple stuff that's still delightfully delicious! Then I can savor the best of both worlds—and not feel like I'm compromising one for the other.

It's my desire that you'll find some heartfelt inspiration within the pages of this book—in addition to some recipes that you can't live without!

We're ecstatic that you'll be joining us as we dive into our favorite dishes—everything from breads, soups and salads, sides, main dishes, cakes and pies, to cookies and bars—and more! All recipes between the covers of this book hold the Mary & Martha stamp of approval—so you know that each and every recipe has been tested in our kitchen before it's been passed on to yours.

Whether you're looking for a family favorite or something new to try, we have dozens of scrumptious selections to choose from. So roll up your sleeves, put on that apron, and. . .

Happy cooking!

MARY & MARTHA

To give our Lord a perfect hospitality,

Mary and Martha must combine.

TERESA OF AVILA

CONTENTS

APPETIZERS

For Starters

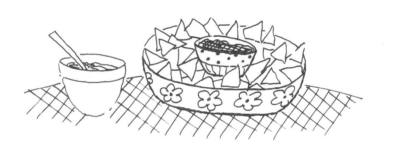

The appetite is sharpened by the first bites.

JOSÉ RIZAL (1861–1896),
Philippine doctor, painter, sculptor,
poet, dramatist, and novelist

Vegetable Roll-Ups

1 (8 OUNCE) PACKAGE CREAM CHEESE

1 (8 OUNCE) PACKAGE SOUR CREAM

1 CUP CHEDDAR CHEESE

1 PACKAGE RANCH DRESSING
      MIX, DRY

½ CUP ONION, CHOPPED

½ CUP CARROTS, CHOPPED

1 CUP BROCCOLI, CHOPPED

1 CUP CAULIFLOWER, CHOPPED

FLOUR TORTILLAS

Mix all ingredients and spread on tortillas. Roll up tight and place in plastic wrap. Refrigerate overnight. When ready to serve, unwrap covering and slice into pinwheels.

Before Mary and I whipped together this cookbook, I had trouble finding my favorite recipes among all the cards and clippings. I purchased a three-ring binder and used plastic photograph sheets with six slots to organize and protect my recipe collection. This is a nifty and inexpensive way to save yourself time in the kitchen.

Bacon Roll-Ups

1 PACKAGE CHICKEN STUFFING MIX

1 CUP CHICKEN BROTH, UNDILUTED

1 PACKAGE BACON

Mix stuffing and chicken broth. Cut bacon slices in half. Spoon stuffing mixture onto each bacon half; roll up and secure. Place on a broiler pan and bake at 350° for 30 minutes. Serve hot.

Tortilla Rolls

2 (8 OUNCE) PACKAGES CREAM CHEESE

1 CUP SOUR CREAM

1 BUNCH GREEN ONIONS, DICED

1 SMALL JAR JALAPEÑO PEPPERS, DICED (OR BLACK OLIVES)

1 PACKAGE FLOUR TORTILLAS

1 JAR PICANTE SAUCE

In a mixing bowl, combine cream cheese, sour cream, onions, and peppers until smooth. Spread a thin layer of mixture onto each tortilla and roll up. Place tortillas in a pan; cover and refrigerate overnight. Cut each roll into bite-sized pieces. Serve with picante sauce for dipping.

Veggie Pizza

2 (8 OUNCE) PACKAGES CRESCENT ROLLS

1 (8 OUNCE) PACKAGE CREAM CHEESE

1 CUP MAYONNAISE

1 ENVELOPE BUTTERMILK RANCH DRESSING MIX, DRY

VEGETABLES OF YOUR CHOICE, CHOPPED

½ CUP CHEDDAR CHEESE, SHREDDED

Pat crescent roll dough out to cover a jelly roll pan. Bake at 375° for 7 minutes. Cool. Blend cream cheese, mayonnaise, and ranch dressing mix. Spread over crust. Top with chopped pieces of your favorite vegetables and shredded cheddar cheese.

The beauty of this dish lies in the option to use the veggies of your choice. If your family members have different tastes, you can split up the toppings on the pizza— half-and-half, or even in quarters. This way everyone will be pleased when it's time to dig in.

Meat and Cheese on Rye

1 POUND GROUND BEEF

1 POUND GROUND SAUSAGE

1 TEASPOON GARLIC POWDER

1 TEASPOON OREGANO

1 TEASPOON WORCESTERSHIRE SAUCE

1 POUND PROCESSED CHEESE, CUBED

1 LOAF PARTY RYE BREAD, SLICED

In a skillet, brown ground beef and sausage; drain. Add garlic powder, oregano, and Worcestershire sauce; mix well. Add cheese. When mixed thoroughly, spread on slices of rye bread. Bake at 350° for 7 to 10 minutes. Serve warm.

This meat and cheese mixture may be made ahead of time and frozen.

Sausage Balls

3 CUPS BISCUIT BAKING MIX

1 POUND SAUSAGE

4 CUPS CHEDDAR CHEESE, SHREDDED

½ CUP PARMESAN CHEESE

½ CUP MILK

½ TEASPOON DRIED ROSEMARY LEAVES

Mix all ingredients together until well blended. Mold into 1-inch balls. Bake at 350° for 20 minutes.

Pizza Spuds

4 POTATOES

½ CUP PIZZA SAUCE

⅔ CUP PEPPERONI, CHOPPED

¼ CUP GRATED PARMESAN CHEESE

¼ CUP MOZZARELLA CHEESE

Poke clean potatoes with a fork. Microwave for 6 minutes. Rotate and turn potatoes; microwave an additional 4 to 6 minutes. Let stand 5 minutes. Slice open potatoes. Spoon in pizza sauce, pepperoni, and cheeses. Microwave for 1 to 2 minutes to melt cheeses.

Teach [God's words] to your children,
talking about them when you sit at home
and when you walk along the road,
when you lie down and when you get up.

DEUTERONOMY 11:19

Party Mix

1 (11 OUNCE) BAG MINI PRETZELS

1 BOX MINI SANDWICH CRACKERS
(CHEESE OR PEANUT BUTTER)

1 CUP DRY-ROASTED PEANUTS

1 CUP SUGAR

½ CUP BUTTER

½ CUP LIGHT CORN SYRUP

2 TABLESPOONS VANILLA

1 TEASPOON BAKING SODA

10 OUNCES CANDY-COATED
CHOCOLATE PIECES
(OR CANDY CORN)

In a large bowl, combine pretzels, sandwich crackers, and peanuts; set aside. In a medium-sized pan, place sugar, butter, and corn syrup. Bring to a boil over medium heat, then add vanilla and baking soda. Pour over pretzel mixture and stir until mixture is coated. Pour into a greased baking pan. Bake at 250° for 45 minutes, stirring every 10 to 15 minutes. Break apart while mixture is still warm then add chocolate candies or candy corn. Store in a sealed container.

This snack mix is perfect for getting your kids involved in the kitchen. Invite them to help you measure and add in the ingredients while you manage the hot oven. It's a win-win situation.... They'll be as proud of their creation as they are delighted to devour it! And you'll enjoy the quality time spent with your kids!

Ranch Crackers

1 PACKAGE RANCH DRESSING MIX, DRY

¾ CUP VEGETABLE OIL

½ TEASPOON GARLIC POWDER

¼ TEASPOON LEMON PEPPER

1 TEASPOON DILL WEED

1 (16 OUNCE) PACKAGE OYSTER CRACKERS

Blend ranch dressing mix, vegetable oil, and spices in a blender and pour over crackers. Stir to mix well. Spread out on a baking sheet and bake at 250° for 20 minutes. Store in an airtight container.

Deviled Eggs

12 EGGS, HARD-BOILED

¼ TEASPOON SALT

½ TEASPOON MUSTARD

1 TEASPOON VINEGAR

½ CUP MAYONNAISE

HAM, MINCED (OPTIONAL)

PAPRIKA

Cut eggs in half lengthwise and remove yolks. In a small mixing bowl, mash yolks and blend in other ingredients. Fill eggs with mixture; sprinkle with paprika. Chill until ready to serve.

A no-mess method for deviling your eggs is to place your filling ingredients in a plastic bag. Massage the bag to mix; then cut a small hole in one corner of the bag. Squeeze the filling out of the bag and directly into the hollows of the egg whites.

Blue Deviled Eggs

A different flavor twist to an old favorite.

12 EGGS

½ CUP (2 OUNCES) BLUE CHEESE, CRUMBLED

1 TABLESPOON PARSLEY

¼ TEASPOON CELERY SEED

¼ TEASPOON PEPPER

⅓ CUP REAL MAYONNAISE

½ TEASPOON HOT SAUCE

In a large saucepan, place eggs in enough water to cover them and bring eggs to a boil. Reduce heat to a slow boil for 12 minutes. Cool and peel eggs. Cut the eggs in half, remove the yolks, and set whites aside. In a small mixing bowl, mash yolks with a fork; stir in the blue cheese, parsley, celery seed, and pepper. Blend mayonnaise and hot sauce; add to yolk mixture, mixing until well blended. Evenly fill the whites. Refrigerate eggs until ready to serve.

Cinnamon Pears

1 LARGE CAN BARTLETT PEAR HALVES

4 TABLESPOONS CINNAMON CANDIES

Drain juice from pears into a small saucepan. Add candies to the juice and cook until candy is dissolved. Remove from heat and place pears back in the juice. As liquid cools, the pears will absorb the red coloring.

*Cinnamon pears make a nice garnish
for a plate or addition to a salad.*

Dried Beef Ball

1 (8 OUNCE) PACKAGE CREAM CHEESE, SOFTENED

¼ CUP GRATED PARMESAN CHEESE

1 TABLESPOON PREPARED HORSERADISH

1 CUP DRIED BEEF, FINELY CUT

Blend cheeses and horseradish; form into a ball. Chill overnight. Roll in dried beef pieces. Serve with assorted crackers.

Hawaiian Cheese Ball

2 (8 OUNCE) PACKAGES CREAM CHEESE, SOFTENED

½ CUP CHEDDAR CHEESE, SHREDDED

1 TEASPOON SEASONED SALT

1 TABLESPOON ONION, FINELY CHOPPED

2 TABLESPOONS GREEN PEPPER, FINELY CHOPPED

1 (8 OUNCE) CAN CRUSHED PINEAPPLE, WELL DRAINED

½ CUP PECANS, FINELY CHOPPED

Blend all ingredients except pecans. Shape into a ball. Chill slightly. Roll ball in pecans. Chill for several hours. Serve with assorted crackers.

Pepperoni Cheese Ball

2 (8 OUNCE) PACKAGES CREAM CHEESE

¼ CUP MAYONNAISE

⅓ CUP GRATED PARMESAN CHEESE

6 OUNCES PEPPERONI, GRATED

Soften cream cheese at room temperature. Mix all ingredients together and shape into a ball. Refrigerate. Allow to soften at room temperature before serving.

This cheese ball seasons better if made a day in advance.

Nacho Dip

1½ CUPS (12 OUNCES) SOUR CREAM

1 (8 OUNCE) PACKAGE CREAM CHEESE, SOFTENED

1 SMALL CONTAINER GRAPE TOMATOES

1 MEDIUM SWEET ONION

1 MEDIUM GREEN PEPPER

1 LARGE CONTAINER TACO SAUCE (MEDIUM SPICE)

2 CUPS CHEDDAR CHEESE, SHREDDED

Mix sour cream and cream cheese; spread in bottom of a container or pie plate. Cut up vegetables; place on top of cream cheese/sour cream mixture. Pour taco sauce over vegetables, then top with cheddar cheese. Refrigerate until ready to serve.

Dips are among my absolute favorite things to whip up. Even the most culinarily challenged can create impossible-to-resist dips that disappear instantly!

Taco Dip

2 (8 OUNCE) PACKAGES CREAM CHEESE, SOFTENED

1 POUND GROUND BEEF

½ MEDIUM ONION, CHOPPED

1 PACKAGE TACO SEASONING

1 BOTTLE TACO SAUCE

1 CUP CHEDDAR CHEESE, SHREDDED

Grease a 2-quart glass baking dish. Spread cream cheese on bottom. On stovetop, cook beef, onion, and dry taco seasoning; drain. Sprinkle meat mixture on cream cheese; top with taco sauce then cheddar cheese. Cover with plastic wrap. Microwave on high for 5 minutes or until bubbly. Serve with nacho chips.

Use an egg slicer to slice olives to place on top of this taco dip. (This tool also works great with slicing strawberries, mushrooms, boiled potatoes, cooked and peeled beets, and much more.)

Salsa Dip

1 (8 OUNCE) PACKAGE CREAM CHEESE
1 LARGE JAR SALSA

Allow cream cheese to soften in a shallow serving bowl. Pour salsa over the rectangle of cream cheese. Serve with tortilla chips.

Spinach Dip

1 PACKAGE VEGETABLE SOUP MIX, DRY
1 (8 OUNCE) CAN WATER CHESTNUTS
1 CUP REAL MAYONNAISE
1½ CUPS SOUR CREAM
1 PACKAGE FROZEN CHOPPED SPINACH, THAWED AND DRAINED

Combine ingredients in order given. Chill. Serve with crackers or pumpernickel bread.

Sherry's Super Easy Crab Dip

1 JAR COCKTAIL SAUCE

1 CAN CRABMEAT, DRAINED

1 (8 OUNCE) PACKAGE CREAM CHEESE

Mix together cocktail sauce and crabmeat; pour over cream cheese. Serve with crackers.

Curry Dip

A light, refreshing taste on veggies.

1 CUP REAL MAYONNAISE

¼ TEASPOON CURRY POWDER

½ TEASPOON TARRAGON VINEGAR

DASH SALT

½ MEDIUM ONION, FINELY CHOPPED (OR ½ TEASPOON ONION POWDER)

Combine all ingredients and chill for 2 hours. Serve with fresh vegetables.

Hot Artichoke Dip

1 (8 OUNCE) PACKAGE CREAM CHEESE, SOFTENED

1 (14 OUNCE) CAN ARTICHOKE HEARTS, DRAINED AND CHOPPED

½ CUP REAL MAYONNAISE

½ CUP GRATED PARMESAN CHEESE

2 TABLESPOONS FRESH BASIL, FINELY CHOPPED

(OR 1 TEASPOON DRIED BASIL LEAVES)

2 TABLESPOONS RED ONION, FINELY CHOPPED

1 CLOVE GARLIC, MINCED

½ CUP TOMATO, CHOPPED

Mix all ingredients except tomato with a mixer on medium speed until well blended. Spoon into a 9-inch pie pan. Bake at 350° for 25 minutes. Sprinkle with tomatoes. Serve with assorted vegetables or toasted Pita Wedges (recipe on page 26).

Tired of preparing the same dishes week after week? Make it a priority to try a new recipe each week. Not only will you expand your culinary skills, chances are there's a new family favorite waiting to make an appearance on your kitchen table.

Ham and Swiss Dip

1 (8 OUNCE) PACKAGE CREAM CHEESE, SOFTENED

⅔ CUP REAL MAYONNAISE

1½ CUPS FULLY COOKED HAM, DICED

1 CUP (4 OUNCES) SWISS CHEESE, SHREDDED

1 TABLESPOON SPICY BROWN MUSTARD

¾ CUP RYE CRACKER CRUMBS

2 TABLESPOONS BUTTER, MELTED

RYE CRACKERS

In a small mixing bowl, beat cream cheese and mayonnaise until smooth. Stir in the ham, cheese, and mustard. Spread in an ungreased 9-inch pie plate. Toss the cracker crumbs in butter; sprinkle over cream cheese mixture. Bake uncovered at 400° for 12 to 15 minutes or until heated through. Serve with rye crackers.

Pita Wedges

3 PITA BREADS

Split pita breads and cut into 8 triangles each. Place on a cookie sheet and bake at 350° for 10 to 12 minutes or until crisp. Serve with Hot Artichoke Dip (recipe on page 25).

BEVERAGES

The Hot and Cold of It

Without the assistance of eating and drinking,

the most sparkling wit would be as heavy

as a bad soufflé, and the brightest talent

as dull as a looking glass on a foggy day.

from *The Modern Housewife*
by ALEXIS SOYER (1810–1858)

Honey-Nut Latte

1 OUNCE HAZELNUT SYRUP
1 OUNCE HONEY
1 TO 2 SHOTS ESPRESSO (APPROXIMATELY 1 TO 2 OUNCES)
STEAMED MILK
WHIPPED TOPPING
HONEY TO TASTE
NUTS, FINELY GROUND

In a large mug, mix hazelnut syrup and honey with espresso; stir until honey dissolves. Fill mug with steamed milk. Garnish with whipped topping, honey, and nuts.

Each one should use whatever gift he has received
to serve others, faithfully administering
God's grace in its various forms.

1 PETER 4:10

Café Mocha

1 OUNCE CHOCOLATE SYRUP

1 SHOT ESPRESSO (APPROXIMATELY 1 OUNCE)

STEAMED MILK

WHIPPED TOPPING

CHOCOLATE SPRINKLES

Place chocolate syrup and espresso in a coffee mug. Fill remainder of coffee mug with steamed milk. Garnish with whipped topping and chocolate sprinkles.

Invite a friend over for coffee or tea. You'll find that the conversation and company will lift your spirit and rejuvenate your soul.

Instant Cappuccino

²/₃ CUP INSTANT COFFEE

1 CUP POWDERED SUGAR

1 CUP POWDERED CHOCOLATE MILK MIX

½ CUP SUGAR

½ TEASPOON CINNAMON

½ TEASPOON NUTMEG

BOILING WATER

Create a fine texture to the instant coffee by putting it through a blender or coffee grinder. Combine all dry ingredients and mix well. Use 1 to 2 heaping tablespoons per cup of boiling water. Store drink mix in an airtight container.

Attach brewing instructions to a jarful of this cappuccino mix and give as a gift to a friend.

Molasses and Cream

1½ CUPS (12 OUNCES) HOT COFFEE

1 TEASPOON MOLASSES

⅛ CUP LIGHT CREAM

Combine coffee and molasses in a large mug; stir until molasses dissolves. Add cream and serve.

Iced Berry Burst

1 (10 OUNCE) PACKAGE FROZEN RASPBERRIES

½ CUP SUGAR

½ CUP WATER

10 CUPS COLD, BREWED COFFEE

1 PINT HALF-AND-HALF

CHIPPED ICE

1 CUP WHIPPED TOPPING

MINT SPRIGS

WHOLE RASPBERRIES

Place frozen raspberries, sugar, and water in a blender and mix until smooth. Strain mixture into a large mixing bowl, eliminating seeds. Add coffee and half-and-half and blend well. Fill chilled glasses half full with chipped ice and pour berry mixture over ice. Garnish with whipped topping, mint sprigs, and whole raspberries.

Tropical Fruit Punch

1 CUP SUGAR

1 CUP WATER

3 CUPS GRAPEFRUIT JUICE

3 CUPS ORANGE JUICE

3 CUPS PINEAPPLE JUICE

½ CUP LEMON JUICE

½ CUP LIME JUICE

1 (2 LITER) BOTTLE GINGER ALE, CHILLED

Combine sugar and water in a saucepan. Heat until boiling. Boil for 2 minutes, stirring constantly. Remove from heat to cool. Pour into a punch bowl and add juices. Cover and refrigerate until ready to serve. Add ginger ale immediately before serving.

Fill ice cube trays with punch (or iced tea, iced coffee, juice, etc.), then freeze. These ice cubes won't water down your beverages.

Slush Punch

4 CUPS SUGAR

WATER

3 SMALL PACKAGES PEACH GELATIN (OR FLAVOR OF YOUR CHOICE)

2 (46 OUNCE) CANS UNSWEETENED PINEAPPLE JUICE

1 TABLESPOON LEMON JUICE

2 LITERS LEMON-LIME SODA, AT ROOM TEMPERATURE

In a saucepan, mix sugar and 4 cups water, then bring to a boil. Let cool. Dissolve gelatin in 3 cups boiling water then add 6 cups cold water. Add the above two mixtures together with the juices. Freeze until solid (approximately 2 days). Remove from freezer 2 to 3 hours before serving and pour the warm lemon-lime soda over top. Mix until slushy.

Give thanks to the LORD, for he is good.

PSALM 136:1

Orange Slush

2 CUPS COLD WATER

2 CUPS SUGAR

1 (6 OUNCE) CAN FROZEN ORANGE JUICE CONCENTRATE

GINGER ALE

In a saucepan, mix water and sugar. Bring to a boil for 2 minutes. Remove from heat and add orange juice concentrate; freeze. Spoon into glasses to serve and pour ginger ale over slush mixture.

Dear heavenly Father, thank You for the gift of friendship. In it we find love, laughter, comfort—too many blessings to name. Please help us to remember that although we don't always see eye to eye with our friends, they help us to broaden our horizons and see things from a new perspective. Amen.

Grape Smoothies

1 PINT VANILLA ICE CREAM, SOFTENED

1 (6 OUNCE) CAN FROZEN GRAPE JUICE CONCENTRATE

1½ CUPS MILK

Combine all ingredients in a blender. Cover and blend until smooth. Serve immediately.

Experiment with different flavors of juice concentrate to create your own original smoothies. Get really crazy...and mix two unique juice concentrates half-and-half with the ice cream and milk. You might just discover a hidden talent while experimenting with these drink concoctions!

BREADS

All Buttered Up

Bread is the king of the table and all else is merely

the court that surrounds the king.

The countries are the soup, the meat, the vegetables,

the salad, but bread is king.

LOUIS BROMFIELD (1896–1956), American novelist

Blueberry-Orange Bread

2 TABLESPOONS BUTTER	**1 CUP SUGAR**
¼ CUP BOILING WATER	**2 CUPS FLOUR**
1 TABLESPOON GRATED ORANGE RIND	**1 TEASPOON BAKING POWDER**
	¼ TEASPOON BAKING SODA
½ CUP ORANGE JUICE	**½ TEASPOON SALT**
1 EGG	**1 CUP FRESH BLUEBERRIES**

SYRUP:

1 TEASPOON GRATED ORANGE RIND	**2 TABLESPOONS FRESH ORANGE JUICE**
2 TABLESPOONS HONEY	

In small bowl, combine butter and boiling water. Add grated orange rind and orange juice; set mixture aside. Beat egg and sugar with mixer until light and fluffy. Combine the flour, baking powder, baking soda, and salt; add to egg mixture alternately with orange juice mixture, beginning and ending with flour mixture. Fold in blueberries. Grease and flour a 9 x 5 x 3-inch loaf pan. Spoon in bread batter. Bake at 350° for 55 minutes. Cool bread in pan for 10 minutes then remove to a wire rack. Combine syrup ingredients; mix well. Spoon over warm bread; let cool.

In the noise and clatter of my kitchen. . .
I possess God in as great tranquillity as if I were on my knees.

BROTHER LAWRENCE (1605–1691),
cook and member of the Discalced Carmelites

Sweet Pecan Roll Rings

2 (8 OUNCE) TUBES REFRIGERATOR
CRESCENT ROLLS

4 TABLESPOONS BUTTER, MELTED
AND DIVIDED

½ CUP PECANS, CHOPPED

¼ CUP SUGAR

1¼ TEASPOONS CINNAMON

½ TEASPOON NUTMEG

½ CUP POWDERED SUGAR

2 TABLESPOONS MAPLE SYRUP

Separate crescent dough into 8 rectangles; seal perforations. Brush rectangles with melted butter. Mix pecans, sugar, cinnamon, and nutmeg; sprinkle mixture over dough and press lightly. Roll dough up jelly-roll style, beginning at the longer end; seal seams. Twist each roll 2 to 3 times. With knife make 6 shallow diagonal slits in each roll. Shape each roll into a ring, pinching ends to seal. Place on a greased baking sheet and brush with remaining butter. Bake at 375° for 12 to 14 minutes or until golden brown. Drizzle combination of powdered sugar and maple syrup over warm rolls.

Make your kitchen time your "God time." Who says you can't talk with God while you're cooking at the stove or while you're standing at the sink rinsing dishes?

Best Cinnamon Sticky Buns

1 CUP BROWN SUGAR, PACKED

½ CUP CORN SYRUP

½ CUP BUTTER

1 CUP PECANS, COARSELY CHOPPED

½ CUP SUGAR

¼ CUP CINNAMON

2 (17.3 OUNCE) TUBES LARGE REFRIGERATOR BISCUITS

Mix brown sugar, corn syrup, and butter in a saucepan. Heat over low to medium heat until sugar dissolves; stir constantly. Add pecans to mixture. Spoon into a greased cake pan. In a shallow bowl, combine sugar and cinnamon. Cut each biscuit in half and dip into cinnamon mixture; place in the cake pan. Bake at 375° for 25 to 30 minutes or until golden brown. Invert pan on platter and serve.

When measuring corn syrup, first spray your measuring cup with cooking oil. The syrup will come out easily, and cleanup will be quicker. This also works well for peanut butter, marshmallow cream, honey, and molasses.

Hawaiian Sweet Bread

¾ CUP SUGAR

½ CUP BUTTER, SOFTENED

1½ TEASPOONS VANILLA

2 EGGS

2 CUPS FLOUR

1 TEASPOON BAKING SODA

½ TEASPOON SALT

1 CUP BANANAS, MASHED

¼ CUP ORANGE JUICE

1 CUP FLAKED COCONUT

¾ CUP MACADAMIA NUTS,
COARSELY CHOPPED

In a large mixing bowl, mix sugar, butter, and vanilla; add eggs. In another large bowl, blend flour, baking soda, and salt; stir into sugar mixture. Use a mixer to beat at low speed for 2 minutes until well blended. Add bananas and orange juice. Continue beating, scraping bowl often, until well mixed. Use a spoon to fold in coconut and nuts. Pour into 1 greased loaf pan or 3 greased mini loaf pans. Bake loaf at 350° for 60 to 65 minutes (mini loaves for 35 to 45 minutes) or until tester comes out clean. Cool for 10 minutes; remove from pan.

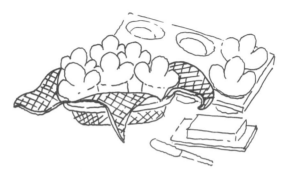

Kansas Muffins

2 CUPS FLOUR

⅓ CUP SUGAR

4 TEASPOONS BAKING POWDER

¼ CUP SHORTENING

MILK

JELLY

DATES, NUTS, OR RAISINS (OPTIONAL)

Sift flour, sugar, and baking powder; cut in shortening. Add just enough milk to make dough drop easily from a spoon. In a paper-lined muffin tin, drop 1 teaspoon of dough then a teaspoon of jelly (mixed with dates, nuts, or raisins if desired), followed by a spoonful of dough to fill the tin ¾ full. Bake at 375° for 25 minutes.

Granny's Zucchini Bread

3 CUPS FLOUR

3 EGGS

1 CUP VEGETABLE OIL

2 CUPS SUGAR

1 TEASPOON VANILLA

2 CUPS ZUCCHINI, PEELED
    AND GRATED

1 CUP WALNUTS, CHOPPED

1 CUP RAISINS

¼ TEASPOON BAKING POWDER

1 TEASPOON CINNAMON

1 TEASPOON SALT

1 TEASPOON BAKING SODA

½ CUP SOUR CREAM

Place flour in a large bowl. Beat eggs and add to flour with remaining ingredients. Beat well for several minutes. Pour into 2 greased loaf pans. Bake at 350° for 55 minutes to 1 hour.

I frequently don't have time to bake for unexpected company. Sweet breads like this one freeze well. When the bread is cool, wrap it tightly in aluminum foil and place the loaf in a plastic freezer bag. Sweet breads will keep in the freezer for several months.

Monkey Bread

1 CUP SUGAR

2 TEASPOONS CINNAMON

3 PACKAGES REFRIGERATOR BISCUITS, CUT INTO QUARTERS

½ CUP NUTS, CHOPPED

½ CUP BUTTER

1 CUP BROWN SUGAR

Place sugar and cinnamon in a large plastic bag. Add biscuits and shake.

Grease a bundt pan. Place coated biscuits in bundt pan with nuts. Boil butter

with sugar for 1 minute; pour over biscuits. Bake at 350° for 30 to 35 minutes.

Remove from bundt pan immediately. This bread is best when served warm.

*Lord, thank You for my home—
and for my kitchen, where I am
able to create tasty meals for my
family. You have provided me with
so much, and often I forget how
blessed I am. I praise You, Lord. Amen.*

Be content with what you have.

HEBREWS 13:5

Sugar Nut Rolls

1 CUP MILK	4½ CUPS FLOUR
½ CUP SUGAR	1¼ CUPS BROWN SUGAR, DIVIDED
1 TEASPOON SALT	1 CUP PECANS, CHOPPED
½ CUP SHORTENING	½ CUP BUTTER, SOFTENED
1 PACKAGE DRY YEAST	1 CUP MAPLE SYRUP, DIVIDED
3 EGGS, BEATEN	

In a saucepan, combine milk, sugar, salt, and shortening; heat mixture until shortening melts. Cool to lukewarm. Add yeast and let stand 20 minutes. In a large mixing bowl, combine milk mixture with eggs; then add flour and beat until dough is smooth and soft. Knead mixture lightly on a floured board. Place in a greased bowl to rise until doubled in size (approximately 1 hour). Grease 3 pans of muffin tins (9 tins each) with butter. Combine ½ cup brown sugar with pecans and divide into each tin. Turn dough out onto floured board and divide into 3 portions. Roll each portion into a long rectangle no more than 3 inches wide and ½ inch thick. Spread the dough with a generous portion of butter blended with ¾ cup brown sugar. Roll dough up starting at the narrow end. Cut into three 1-inch slices and place one in each tin. Let rise. Cover each slice with ½ teaspoon maple syrup. Bake at 400° for 25 minutes.

Mom's Gingerbread

½ CUP BUTTER

1 CUP SUGAR

1 CUP MOLASSES

⅔ CUP MILK

2 EGGS

¼ TEASPOON SALT

3 CUPS FLOUR

2 TEASPOONS BAKING SODA

2 TEASPOONS CINNAMON

2 TEASPOONS GINGER

WHIPPED TOPPING

Mix all ingredients together; pour into a greased loaf pan. Bake at 325° until loaf springs back when lightly touched (approximately 45 minutes). Serve plain or with whipped topping.

I always take care of cleaning up the kitchen directly after a meal so I can sit down with a clear conscience. Often I start a sink full of soapy water even while I'm still cooking and wash up my utensils between preparations. I've even been known to clean the kitchen while my family finishes eating. I just can't let myself relax with a messy kitchen.

You place way too much emphasis on cleanup, Martha. Don't worry about having a spotless kitchen while you have guests. The dishes can always wait until later. Besides, no one will remember your messy kitchen, but they will remember time spent with you.

Poppy Seed Bread

3 CUPS FLOUR

2$\frac{1}{4}$ CUPS SUGAR

1$\frac{1}{2}$ CUPS MILK

1$\frac{1}{8}$ CUPS VEGETABLE OIL

3 EGGS

1$\frac{1}{2}$ TEASPOONS POPPY SEEDS

1$\frac{1}{2}$ TEASPOONS SALT

1$\frac{1}{2}$ TEASPOONS BAKING POWDER

1$\frac{1}{2}$ TEASPOONS ALMOND FLAVORING

1$\frac{1}{2}$ TEASPOONS BUTTER FLAVORING

Mix all ingredients. Pour into 2 greased loaf pans. Bake at 350° for 1 hour. Cool for 5 to 10 minutes then remove bread from pans.

GLAZE:

$\frac{3}{4}$ CUP SUGAR

$\frac{1}{4}$ CUP ORANGE JUICE

$\frac{1}{2}$ TEASPOON BUTTER FLAVORING

$\frac{1}{2}$ TEASPOON VANILLA

$\frac{1}{2}$ TEASPOON ALMOND FLAVORING

Mix all ingredients and pour over hot bread.

Pull-Apart
Cheesy Mushroom Bread

1 LOAF FRENCH BREAD

1 POUND BABY SWISS CHEESE, SLICED

1 LARGE CAN SLICED MUSHROOMS, DRAINED

1½ TO 2 STICKS BUTTER

¼ CUP ONION, CHOPPED

2 TEASPOONS POPPY SEEDS

½ TEASPOON DRY MUSTARD

Cut 3 slits lengthwise into bread, down to bottom crust. Stuff with Baby Swiss cheese slices and mushrooms. Place bread on aluminum foil. Melt butter; add chopped onions, poppy seeds, and dry mustard. Pour over bread. Wrap bread in foil and bake at 350° for 40 minutes. Slice before serving.

Baking Powder Biscuits

2 CUPS FLOUR, SIFTED

4 TEASPOONS BAKING POWDER

1 SCANT TEASPOON SALT

1 TEASPOON SUGAR

5 TABLESPOONS SHORTENING

¾ CUP MILK

Sift dry ingredients together. Cut in shortening; then add milk all at once. Stir with a fork until mixture begins to leave sides of bowl. Turn out onto a board and knead for 30 seconds. Roll out to ½ inch thick. Cut and place in a baking pan. Bake at 425° for 15 minutes.

Enhance a plain roll or slice of bread with extra flavor. Soften a stick of butter, then whip in your choice of garlic, rosemary, lemon juice, or honey. Be creative!

Buttermilk Biscuits

½ CUP COLD BUTTER

2 CUPS FLOUR

3 TEASPOONS BAKING POWDER

¼ TEASPOON SALT

¾ CUP BUTTERMILK

In a mixing bowl, use a pastry blender to cut butter into a blend of flour, baking powder, and salt. Stir in buttermilk with a fork until batter is just moistened. Turn dough out onto a lightly floured board and knead lightly 4 to 5 times. Pat dough by hand out into a circle ¾ inch thick. Cut with a round biscuit cutter. Place biscuits on a greased baking pan. Bake at 450° for 8 to 10 minutes.

I make these biscuits often, so I've started premeasuring all the dry ingredients and placing enough for one recipe in individual bags for easy preparation later.

*I took advantage of Martha's great
tip and started premeasuring
and canning dry ingredients for my
best-tasting recipes. I then attach
cards with pretty ribbon that explain
the additional ingredients needed
and directions for baking and give
them away as gifts. My friends and
family are delighted to receive these
simple, but delicious, treats. To add
an extra-special touch, include a
personal note on the card.*

Cheddar Biscuits

1¼ POUNDS BISCUIT BAKING MIX

3 OUNCES CHEDDAR CHEESE, SHREDDED

1⅓ CUPS WATER

1 TEASPOON GARLIC POWDER

¼ TEASPOON SALT

⅛ TEASPOON ONION POWDER

½ CUP BUTTER, MELTED

⅛ TEASPOON DRIED PARSLEY FLAKES

Grease a baking sheet. In a mixing bowl, combine baking mix, cheese, water,

garlic powder, salt, and onion powder, forming a stiff dough. Drop by spoonfuls

onto the baking sheet. Bake at 375° for 10 to 12 minutes. Combine butter and

parsley, and brush over browned biscuits while still warm.

Buttery Breadsticks

2¼ CUPS FLOUR

3½ TEASPOONS BAKING POWDER

1 CUP MILK

1 TABLESPOON SUGAR

1½ TEASPOONS SALT

⅓ CUP BUTTER, MELTED

Stir flour, baking powder, milk, sugar, and salt together with fork until dough clings. Turn out onto a floured board and knead lightly about 10 times. Roll out into a rectangle ½ inch thick. With a floured knife, cut dough in half lengthwise, then crosswise into 16 strips. Dip each strip in butter on both sides. Bake on a cookie sheet at 450° for 15 to 20 minutes.

Rejoice in the Lord always. I will say it again: Rejoice!

PHILIPPIANS 4:4

Corn Bread

1 CUP FLOUR

1 CUP CORNMEAL

1 TEASPOON SALT

2 TABLESPOONS SUGAR

3 TABLESPOONS BAKING POWDER

1 CUP MILK

2 EGGS, BEATEN

3 TABLESPOONS BUTTER, MELTED AND COOLED

Combine dry ingredients; add milk, eggs, and butter. Mix until fairly smooth.

Bake in a greased 8 x 8-inch pan at 425° for 20 to 25 minutes.

Before heading out to the grocery store, be sure to check your pantry. Take a look and see what you're low on; and if you've planned a weekly supper menu, review that, as well. Be sure to write everything you need on your grocery list, rather than just make a mental note of it. As you go through the store, cross off items on your list as you place them in the cart. While this may seem like a lot of trouble for some of you, this definitely cuts down on those "Oh no, I forgot _____ (fill in the blank)!" moments. You know we've all been there!

Corn Skillet Fritters

1 CUP FLOUR

1 TABLESPOON SUGAR

1 TEASPOON SALT

1 TEASPOON BAKING POWDER

½ CUP MILK

2 EGG YOLKS

2 TABLESPOONS BUTTER, MELTED

2 CUPS WHOLE KERNEL CORN, DRAINED

2 EGG WHITES, STIFFLY BEATEN

VEGETABLE OIL

MAPLE SYRUP

Sift dry ingredients together; set aside. In a mixing bowl, combine milk, egg yolks, butter, and corn. Add dry ingredients. Fold in beaten egg whites. Drop batter by spoonfuls into hot oil (1 inch deep) in a skillet. Cook until golden brown (3 to 4 minutes). Serve hot with maple syrup.

A good trick for separating egg white from the yolk is to break the egg into a funnel over a small bowl. The white will pass through the funnel while the yolk remains suspended at the top of the funnel.

Garlic Bread Loaf

3 TABLESPOONS BUTTER

2 CLOVES GARLIC, MINCED

2 CANS REFRIGERATOR BISCUITS

2 TO 3 TABLESPOONS GRATED PARMESAN AND/OR ROMANO CHEESE

Melt 1 tablespoon of butter and pour into bottom of a loaf pan. Melt
remaining butter with garlic. Lay one log of biscuits on each side of the pan.
Fan out biscuits and drizzle garlic butter over the top, in between, and around
the sides. Scatter cheese over top and in between biscuits. Bake at 350° for 30
minutes or until center is solid. Serve warm, pulling apart the sections.

Linda Germany's Yeast Bread

½ CUP BUTTER

2 CUPS MILK

2 PACKAGES DRY YEAST

1 TABLESPOON SUGAR

1 CUP WATER

2 EGGS

2½ TEASPOONS SALT

½ CUP SUGAR

7 TO 8 CUPS FLOUR

Melt butter in milk on low heat (don't scald). Dissolve yeast and 1 tablespoon sugar in water. Mix eggs, salt, and ½ cup sugar. Add buttery milk and liquid yeast. Gradually work in the flour, kneading until elastic and velvety. Let rise for 30 minutes, then knead again. Let rise for 1 hour and form into 4 loaves. Let rise for an additional 1 to 2 hours and bake at 350° for 25 to 30 minutes.

It may sound odd, but I've found that the dishwasher is a great place for letting bread dough rise. Place dough in a bowl and cover with a towel. Set the bowl on the bottom rack of the dishwasher, then set the dishwasher to the dry heat cycle. The warm, moist air is perfect for a quick rise.

Refrigerator Rolls

1 PACKAGE QUICK YEAST

½ CUP WARM WATER

1 TEASPOON SUGAR

½ CUP SHORTENING

½ CUP SUGAR

1 EGG, BEATEN UNTIL LIGHT IN COLOR

2 CUPS LUKEWARM WATER

2 TEASPOONS SALT

6 CUPS FLOUR (APPROXIMATE MEASUREMENT)

Blend yeast, ½ cup warm water, and 1 teaspoon sugar; let stand for 15 to 30 minutes. Cream together shortening and ½ cup sugar. Add egg, water, yeast mixture, and salt. Stiffen dough by mixing in ½ cup flour at a time. Turn dough out onto a board and knead as for bread. Allow to rise once in greased bowl until doubled in bulk. Work down and store in the refrigerator until ready to bake (no more than 2 days). Two to three hours before serving, bring dough out and knead. Place in a greased bowl and let rise until doubled in bulk. Form dough into rolls. Bake at 375° for 20 minutes.

CANDIES

Sweet Temptations

If you are not feeling well, if you have not slept,

chocolate will revive you.

But you have no chocolate!

I think of that again and again!

My dear, how will you ever manage?

MARQUISE DE SÉVIGNÉ (1626–1696), French writer

Wonder Fudge

¼ CUP MARGARINE

1 (12 OUNCE) PACKAGE SEMISWEET CHOCOLATE CHIPS

¼ CUP CORN SYRUP

1 TEASPOON VANILLA

1½ CUPS POWDERED SUGAR, SIFTED

2 CUPS CRISP RICE CEREAL

Mix margarine, chocolate chips, corn syrup, and vanilla in a large saucepan. Cook over very low heat, stirring constantly until smooth. Remove from heat. Add powered sugar and crisp rice cereal. Stir until cereal is evenly coated. Press mixture into buttered square cake pan. Refrigerate until firm. Cut into squares.

Fudge doesn't like to come out of the pan, so I've learned to line my pans with either aluminum foil or waxed paper. Form the foil to your pan, then pour in the fudge. When fudge is cooled, you can easily lift it from the pan and place it on a cutting board to cut into squares.

Almond Florentines

1 CUP BUTTER (MARGARINE WILL NOT SUFFICE)
1 CUP SUGAR
⅓ CUP HONEY

⅓ CUP HEAVY WHIPPING CREAM
4 CUPS SLICED BLANCHED ALMONDS
6 OUNCES SEMISWEET CHOCOLATE CHIPS

Spray five 8-inch aluminum foil pie tins with cooking oil. Melt butter in large saucepan. Add sugar, honey, and whipping cream. Bring to a boil over medium heat. Stir frequently. When the boil creates a wild froth on top, stir constantly and allow to continue to boil at this level for exactly 90 seconds. Remove saucepan from heat. Add almonds. Quickly pour mixture into the pie tins. Bake at 350° for 10 to 14 minutes until rich golden brown (most likely will be bubbling). Cool in pan for 20 minutes; then refrigerate in pan for 30 minutes. Turn out onto waxed paper; stack in refrigerator with waxed paper in between the florentines. Melt chocolate and spread on the bottom of the florentines. Let cool. Break into bark. Store in the refrigerator with plastic wrap between layers.

Find you're often distressed over a messy kitchen? Instead of focusing on the yucky part of cleanup, remember that the dirty pots and pans, the sticky table, the crumbs on the floor…all mean that you have a family who needs your love and care. Now doesn't that just make it all worthwhile?

Toffee

1 POUND BUTTER

2 CUPS SUGAR

1 (6 OUNCE) PACKAGE SEMISWEET CHOCOLATE CHIPS, MELTED

Bring butter and sugar to a boil—to 310° on candy thermometer. Pour mixture out onto a greased cookie sheet and place in the refrigerator to cool. Break into pieces and dip in melted chocolate. Place on waxed paper until chocolate hardens.

Buckeyes

1 POUND BUTTER

2 CUPS PEANUT BUTTER

2½ POUNDS POWDERED SUGAR

3 TEASPOONS VANILLA

6 OUNCES SEMISWEET CHOCOLATE CHIPS

¼ POUND PARAFFIN WAX

Cream butter and peanut butter; add powdered sugar and mix well; add vanilla. Use hands to blend. Consistency should be ready for shaping into balls the size of large marbles. Melt chocolate and paraffin in a small double boiler. Rest a ball of peanut butter mixture between prongs of a 2-pronged meat fork and dip into chocolate to coat all but the top. Place on waxed paper in the refrigerator to solidify.

Caramel Corn

1½ CUPS POPCORN

1 CUP CORN SYRUP

1 CUP BROWN SUGAR

2 CUPS SUGAR

½ CUP BUTTER

3 TEASPOONS VINEGAR

1 TEASPOON SALT

1 TEASPOON BAKING SODA

Pop corn and set aside. In a large saucepan, combine all but the popcorn and baking soda, and cook to hard crack stage. Test readiness in a cup of ice water (should separate into hard but flexible threads). Remove from heat and add baking soda. Pour over popped corn; stir well to coat.

Chocolate Chip Cheese Ball

1 (8 OUNCE) PACKAGE CREAM CHEESE, SOFTENED

2½ TABLESPOONS BROWN SUGAR

½ TEASPOON VANILLA

1 STICK BUTTER (NOT MARGARINE)

¾ CUP POWDERED SUGAR

1 (12 OUNCE) BAG MINI CHOCOLATE CHIPS

¾ CUP PECANS, CHOPPED

VANILLA WAFERS OR GRAHAM CRACKERS

In a mixing bowl, use mixer to blend cream cheese, brown sugar, vanilla, and butter until whipped; stir in powdered sugar and chocolate chips. Refrigerate for at least 2 hours before forming into a ball-type shape. Coat ball with pecans and refrigerate for 1 additional hour. Serve with vanilla wafers or graham crackers.

Delight yourself in the LORD
and he will give you the desires of your heart.

PSALM 37:4

Chocolate Pretzel Rings

4 DOZEN PRETZEL CIRCLES

1 (8 OUNCE) PACKAGE MILK CHOCOLATE KISSES, UNWRAPPED

50 (APPROXIMATELY ½ CUP) CANDY-COATED CHOCOLATE PIECES

Cover a cookie sheet with waxed paper. Spread pretzels out on the sheet. Place a chocolate kiss in the center of each pretzel. Bake at 275° for 2 to 3 minutes—until chocolate is softened. Immediately place a coated candy on each chocolate and press down slightly, so that chocolate spreads to touch pretzel. Refrigerate until chocolate is firm. Store at room temperature.

These easy-to-make pretzel rings always win over my stressed-out friends. I place these in a resealable bag and include them in a gift basket with various items that lend themselves to indulgence— bubble bath, a good book, a scented candle... Then I attach a card that simply reads, "Enjoy! You deserve a little 'me' time!"

Cookie Truffles

These are easy to make and look great!

1 (1 POUND) PACKAGE CHOCOLATE SANDWICH COOKIES, CRUSHED

1 (8 OUNCE) PACKAGE CREAM CHEESE, SOFTENED

1 POUND CHOCOLATE CANDY COATING, MELTED

¼ CUP WHITE CANDY COATING OR WHITE CHOCOLATE CHIPS, MELTED

In a large mixing bowl, combine crushed cookies and cream cheese to form a stiff dough. Shape into balls; then with a fork, dip into melted chocolate candy coating. Place on a wire rack over waxed paper in a cool area until set. Melt the white chocolate in a plastic bag, cut a tiny hole in one corner, and drizzle chocolate over the top of each candy ball.

While Martha is able to make cookie truffles look as good as they taste, I've always struggled to make them look pretty. The funny thing is, though, they always taste like a dream—no matter if they look like mangled blobs of chocolate. Don't fret if the turnout of this confection isn't what you'd like it to be. Always remember that in the kitchen, taste—not appearance—is everything.

Microwave Peanut Brittle

1 CUP SUGAR

½ CUP WHITE CORN SYRUP

1 CUP PEANUTS, ROASTED AND SALTED

1 TEASPOON BUTTER

1 TEASPOON VANILLA

1 TEASPOON BAKING SODA

In a 1½-quart microwave-safe casserole dish, combine sugar and corn syrup. Microwave on high for 4 minutes, stirring every minute. Add nuts and microwave for 3½ minutes. Add butter and vanilla and microwave for 1½ minutes. Add baking soda and stir gently until foamy. Pour out onto a jelly roll pan to cool. Break into pieces.

Puppy Chow

1 (12 OUNCE) PACKAGE CHOCOLATE CHIPS

½ CUP BUTTER

1 CUP PEANUT BUTTER

1 BOX CRISP CORN CEREAL

1 POUND POWDERED SUGAR, DIVIDED

Melt chocolate chips, butter, and peanut butter together. Stir in cereal and coat well. Put half of the mixture in a large paper bag with half the powdered sugar. Shake well; repeat with second half. Store in covered container.

Here's a little quote about Mary's kitchen...

"A messy kitchen is a happy kitchen, and this kitchen is delirious."

(UNKNOWN)

Oh, Martha, I think you're delirious!

Stix and Stones Candy Mix

2 CUPS MINI PRETZEL STICKS

4 CUPS TOASTED OATS CEREAL

4 CUPS CRISP CORN OR RICE SQUARES CEREAL

1 CUP SALTED PEANUTS OR MIXED NUTS

1 POUND WHITE CHOCOLATE COATING (ALMOND BARK)

$\frac{1}{2}$ TO 1 POUND CANDY-COATED CHOCOLATE PIECES

In a large bowl, combine pretzels, cereal, and nuts. In a large glass bowl, melt coating chunks in the microwave, stirring every 30 seconds until smooth. Pour over pretzels, cereal, and nuts and mix well. Fold in coated chocolate pieces last. Spread mixture over 2 to 3 waxed paper–lined baking sheets. Cool and break apart. Store in an airtight container.

CONDIMENTS

Savor the Flavor

Cookery is not chemistry.

It is an art.

It requires instinct and taste

rather than exact measurements.

X. MARCEL BOULESTIN (1878–1943), chef and food writer

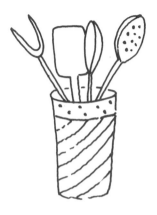

Hot Pepper Butter

50 HOT PEPPERS, SEEDS REMOVED

1 QUART YELLOW MUSTARD

1 QUART WHITE VINEGAR

5 CUPS SUGAR

1 TABLESPOON SALT

1½ CUPS FLOUR

1 PINT WATER

Grind peppers in a blender. Place hot peppers, mustard, vinegar, sugar, and salt in a saucepan and bring to a boil. Add flour and water. Cook until mixture thickens. Place in sterilized jars and seal.

Barbecue Relish

The relish is a must on hot dogs and sausage.

15 GREEN TOMATOES

6 RED PEPPERS

6 GREEN PEPPERS

6 LARGE CARROTS

6 ONIONS

1 CUP SALT

Clean vegetables and remove stems. Cut into large chunks. Grind all vegetables and place in a large crock. Cover with water and add salt. Let stand in salt water overnight. Drain.

Sauce:

3 CUPS VINEGAR

4 CUPS SUGAR

1 TEASPOON GROUND CLOVES

1 TEASPOON TURMERIC

1 CUP WATER

1 TABLESPOON MUSTARD SEED

1 TEASPOON CINNAMON

Blend all sauce ingredients and pour over drained vegetables. Cook in a large saucepan over medium heat for 45 minutes. Seal in sterilized pint jars.

Colored Cucumber Pickles

Tasty and pretty. These are a colorful addition to any holiday relish tray.

2 GALLONS (APPROXIMATELY 7 POUNDS) EXTRA LARGE CUCUMBERS, PEELED, CORED, AND SLICED ½ INCH THICK

WATER

2 CUPS LIME JUICE

7 CUPS VINEGAR, DIVIDED

1 TABLESPOON ALUM

1 BOTTLE RED OR GREEN FOOD COLORING

10 CUPS SUGAR

8 CINNAMON STICKS

In a large bowl or crock, soak cucumbers in 2 gallons of water with lime juice for 24 hours. Drain and rinse well; place in a large saucepan. Combine 1 cup vinegar, alum, and food coloring; pour over cucumbers and add water to cover the cucumbers. Heat on the stovetop and simmer for 2 hours. Drain and place in a bowl. Make a syrup with 6 cups vinegar, 2 cups water, sugar, and cinnamon sticks; bring to a boil. Pour syrup over the cucumbers and let stand overnight. Drain and reheat syrup; pour back over cucumbers and let stand overnight. Repeat for 3 days. On the third day, pack cucumbers with syrup in sterilized pint jars and seal.

Dandelion Blossom Jelly

1 QUART DANDELION BLOSSOMS

5 CUPS WATER

1 PACKAGE FRUIT PECTIN

4 CUPS SUGAR

Wash and remove all green from dandelion blossoms. Place water and blossoms in a large saucepan; boil for 5 minutes then drain, retaining liquid. Add fruit pectin and sugar to liquid. Cook until thickened (should coat a spoon).

Many items in this section of our book are great giveaways for your friends and family. A jar of homemade preserves is quite a treat for those who don't have much time to spend in the kitchen. And something unusual like Dandelion Blossom Jelly makes for a doubly appreciated treat.

Yellow Tomato Preserves

8 POUNDS PEAR-SHAPED YELLOW
   TOMATOES
2 LEMONS, THINLY SLICED WITH
   SEEDS REMOVED

1½ QUARTS WATER
6 POUNDS SUGAR
4 TO 6 PIECES GINGER ROOT

Wash tomatoes and leave skins on; or, if desired, scald and remove skins. Cook lemons for approximately 20 minutes in 1 pint water. Boil remaining water and sugar to make a syrup; add the tomatoes, ginger root, and the cooked lemon rind and liquid. Boil until tomatoes are somewhat clear and the syrup thick. Remove the filmy covering and pour the preserves into hot sterilized glass jars. Seal and store in a cool, dry place.

Nutmeg Sauce

2 TABLESPOONS SUGAR
2 TABLESPOONS CORNSTARCH
1 TABLESPOON BUTTER

1 CUP WATER
DROP OF ALMOND FLAVORING
SPRINKLE OF NUTMEG

Combine ingredients in a medium saucepan.
Cook over medium heat until thickened.

*Serve this warm sauce over
pound cake or gingerbread.*

Poppy Seed Salad Dressing

2 CUPS OIL

⅔ CUP VINEGAR

1½ CUPS SUGAR

1 TABLESPOON ONION, CHOPPED

1 TABLESPOON MUSTARD

1 TEASPOON SALT

⅛ CUP POPPY SEEDS

Mix in a blender until smooth. Keep refrigerated until ready to use on a salad.

Pickled Beets

WHOLE BEETS, COOKED AND PEELED

BROWN SUGAR

VINEGAR

1 TABLESPOON PICKLING SPICE

Cut up cooked beets and pack into sterilized jars. Make a syrup with equal parts brown sugar and vinegar. Season with pickling spice. Fill canning jars ½ inch from the top with syrup. Seal jars.

DESSERTS
Happy Endings

Young children and chickens would ever be eating.

from *Points of Huswifery* by THOMAS TUSSER (1524–1580)

CAKES

Nowhere is the stomach of the traveler or visitor put in such constant peril as among the cake-inventive housewives and daughters of New England. Such is the universal attention paid to this particular branch of epicurism in these states, that I greatly suspect that some of the Pilgrim Fathers must have come over to the country with the Cookery *book under one arm and the Bible under the other.*

CHARLES JOSEPH LATROBE (1801–1875),
traveler and author

Cottage Cheese Cake

This recipe from Hungary is delish! Though the combination sounds odd, it's become a family favorite. Mary is asked to bring this delightful dessert to every family gathering.

1 LARGE CONTAINER SMALL CURD COTTAGE CHEESE	1 CUP SUGAR
	CINNAMON
4 EGGS	DILL

CRUST:

2 CUPS FLOUR	⅔ CUP SHORTENING
1 TEASPOON SALT	5 TO 7 TABLESPOONS COLD WATER

Mix together cottage cheese, eggs, and sugar in a large mixing bowl. Set aside.

Prepare crust: Mix together flour, salt, and shortening with a fork. Add water.

Roll out crust to fit a cookie sheet. Fill crust with cottage cheese mixture. Sprinkle cinnamon and dill on top. Bake at 375° for 45 minutes. Cool; cut into squares.

Baking products can be expensive, and you don't want anything to go to waste. If you don't bake very often or like to buy your baking ingredients in bulk, you can keep many products like baking chocolate, baking chips, flour, nuts, dried fruits, butter, marshmallows, and cream cheese in the freezer until you are ready to use them.

Chocolate Zucchini Cake

1 CUP BROWN SUGAR

½ CUP SUGAR

½ CUP MARGARINE

½ CUP VEGETABLE OIL

3 EGGS

1 TEASPOON VANILLA

½ CUP BUTTERMILK

2½ CUPS FLOUR

½ TEASPOON ALLSPICE

½ TEASPOON CINNAMON

½ TEASPOON SALT

2 TEASPOONS BAKING SODA

¼ CUP COCOA

1¾ CUPS SHREDDED ZUCCHINI, DRAINED

1 CUP SEMISWEET CHOCOLATE CHIPS

Cream brown sugar, sugar, margarine, and vegetable oil. Add eggs, vanilla, buttermilk, and flour; stir well. Sift allspice, cinnamon, salt, baking soda, and cocoa together, then sift into other ingredients; beat well. Stir in zucchini and pour into a cake pan. Sprinkle chocolate chips on top. Bake at 325° for 45 minutes.

If you prepare your pan with flour, you could end up with an unsightly white residue on your cake. Try dusting pans with cocoa instead of flour when you're baking a chocolate dessert.

Chocolate Toffee Bar Cake

1 GERMAN CHOCOLATE
  CAKE MIX

1 CAN SWEETENED CONDENSED
  MILK

1 JAR CARAMEL ICE CREAM
  TOPPING

1 (8 OUNCE) TUB WHIPPED
  TOPPING

3 TO 6 MILK CHOCOLATE TOFFEE
  CANDY BARS, CRUSHED

Bake cake according to package directions. While cake is still hot, poke holes in cake about 1 inch apart, using the handle of a wooden spoon. Combine milk and caramel topping; pour over cake, completely covering it. Refrigerate cake overnight. Before serving, cover cake with whipped topping and sprinkle with candy bar crumbs.

*A simple gift idea for someone special:
Insert a coupon for one of your
signature desserts inside a card. For example...*

TO SOMEONE SPECIAL:

Coupon for my homemade _____ (fill in the blank with dessert of your choice), for you to redeem and enjoy when you wish. Never expires!

With love, _____ (your signature here)

Ice Water Chocolate Cake

¾ CUP MARGARINE

2¼ CUPS SUGAR

1½ TEASPOONS VANILLA

3 EGGS

3 SQUARES CHOCOLATE, MELTED

3 CUPS FLOUR

1½ TEASPOONS BAKING SODA

¾ TEASPOON SALT

1½ CUPS ICE WATER

Blend together margarine, sugar, and vanilla until mixture resembles consistency of whipping cream. Add 3 eggs, one at a time, then chocolate. Sift together flour, baking soda, and salt; add to creamy mixture alternately with ice water. Place in a greased 9 x 13-inch cake pan and bake at 350° for 45 minutes.

Icebox Cake

8 WHOLE GRAHAM CRACKERS

1 SMALL PACKAGE INSTANT CHOCOLATE PUDDING

2 CUPS MILK

Break graham crackers into pieces to line a 9 x 5-inch loaf pan. (You should have enough crackers for 3 layers.) Place one layer of crackers in the pan. Set the remaining crackers aside. Using the milk, prepare the pudding according to the package instructions. After mixing, work quickly so pudding doesn't set up. Pour about ⅓ of the pudding into the prepared pan, spreading it out evenly. Place a layer of graham crackers on the pudding. Pour another ⅓ of the pudding in, spreading evenly. Place the final layer of graham crackers and top with the remaining pudding. Cover and chill overnight. To serve, cut into pieces, using a spatula to place on dessert dishes.

For a richer, creamier pudding, I use canned evaporated milk instead of regular whole milk.

Red Devil's Food Cake

½ CUP SHORTENING

1¾ CUPS SUGAR, DIVIDED

1 TEASPOON VANILLA

3 EGG YOLKS

2½ CUPS FLOUR, SIFTED

½ CUP COCOA POWDER

1½ TEASPOONS BAKING SODA

1 TEASPOON SALT

1⅓ CUPS COLD WATER

3 EGG WHITES

SEA FOAM FROSTING

Cream shortening and 1 cup sugar until light. Add vanilla and egg yolks one at a time, beating well after each addition. Sift together flour, cocoa powder, baking soda, and salt; add to creamed mixture alternately with water (beating after each addition). Beat egg whites to soft peaks; gradually add ¾ cup sugar, then beat to stiff peaks. Fold into batter; blend well. Pour into 2 greased and lightly floured round layer cake pans. Bake at 350° for 35 to 40 minutes. Cool and ice with Sea Foam frosting (can be purchased at your local supermarket).

Have you ever created a mess when you've tried to cover a frosted cake? I've discovered that when I don't have a raised cover for my cake pan, I can lay a paper towel over it. The frosting will stick at first, but soon the oils in the frosting will soak into the towel, and when you are ready to remove the paper towel, your frosting won't be pulled from the cake.

Mandarin Orange–Pineapple Cake

1 YELLOW CAKE MIX

¾ CUP OIL

3 EGGS

1 SMALL CAN MANDARIN ORANGES WITH JUICE

Combine cake ingredients. Bake in two 9-inch round pans at 350° for 25 minutes. When cool, cut into 4 layers using dental floss.

ICING:

16 OUNCES WHIPPED TOPPING

1 LARGE PACKAGE INSTANT VANILLA PUDDING

1 (16 OUNCE) CAN CRUSHED PINEAPPLE WITH JUICE

Fold together icing ingredients. Ice cake layers and stack. Tastes best if this cake sets for 24 hours before serving.

Dump-It Cake

1 (20 OUNCE) CAN CRUSHED PINEAPPLE

1 (21 OUNCE) CAN CHERRY PIE FILLING

1 YELLOW CAKE MIX

½ CUP PECANS, CHOPPED (OPTIONAL)

¾ CUP BUTTER, SLICED

Spread pineapple with juice in a cake pan; layer cherry pie filling on top. Sprinkle yellow cake mix over pie filling layer—do not mix or stir. Arrange pecans on top. Dot with butter and bake at 350° for 50 to 55 minutes.

A simple kindness, like baking an extra cake and giving it away to a neighbor, has the potential to make a big impact. Reaching out to others with your culinary creations leaves lasting imprints on hearts.

But the fruit of the Spirit is love, joy, peace, patience, kindness, goodness, faithfulness, gentleness and self-control.

GALATIANS 5:22–23

Pineapple Sheet Cake

2 CUPS FLOUR

2 CUPS SUGAR

2 EGGS

2 TEASPOONS VANILLA

2 TEASPOONS BAKING SODA

20 OUNCES CRUSHED PINEAPPLE
WITH JUICE

1 CUP WALNUTS, CHOPPED

Combine and mix cake ingredients. Bake on a greased cookie sheet at 350° for 20 to 25 minutes.

ICING:

1 (8 OUNCE) PACKAGE CREAM
CHEESE, SOFTENED

½ CUP BUTTER

2 CUPS POWDERED SUGAR

2 TEASPOONS VANILLA

Combine icing ingredients and mix until creamy. Top with additional chopped walnuts if desired.

Another trick for dusting cake pans is to use sugar instead of flour. The mild sweet coating on the cake is more appealing than lumpy flour.

Luscious Cheesecake

CRUST:

1 CUP GRAHAM CRACKER CRUMBS   ½ CUP BUTTER, MELTED

FILLING:

4 (8 OUNCE) PACKAGES CREAM   1 TEASPOON VANILLA
    CHEESE   1 CUP SUGAR
3 TABLESPOONS LEMON JUICE   6 MEDIUM-SIZED EGGS

TOPPING:

24 OUNCES SOUR CREAM   ½ CUP SUGAR

Mix together crust ingredients and pat into the bottom of a greased 9-inch spring form pan. Beat cream cheese for filling. Gradually add lemon juice, vanilla, and sugar. Add eggs one at a time, stirring after each addition. Pour over top of crust. Place baking pan on top of a cookie sheet and bake at 325° for 35 to 40 minutes. When done, set oven at 450° and mix together topping ingredients; spoon on top of cheesecake and bake an additional 5 to 10 minutes, until topping becomes bubbly. Cool; refrigerate overnight until ready to serve.

Peanut Butter Coffee Cake

2 CUPS FLOUR

1 CUP BROWN SUGAR, PACKED

2 TEASPOONS BAKING POWDER

½ TEASPOON BAKING SODA

¼ TEASPOON SALT

1 CUP MILK

½ CUP CREAMY PEANUT BUTTER

2 EGGS

¼ CUP BUTTER

TOPPING:

½ CUP BROWN SUGAR, PACKED

½ CUP FLOUR

¼ CUP CREAMY PEANUT BUTTER

3 TABLESPOONS BUTTER

In a large bowl, add flour, brown sugar, baking powder, baking soda, and salt. Then add milk, peanut butter, eggs, and butter. Beat with an electric mixer on low until blended. Then turn mixer to high and beat for 3 minutes, while scraping sides of bowl frequently. Pour into a greased cake pan and spread evenly. Mix topping ingredients until crumbly; sprinkle over cake mixture. Bake at 375° for 30 minutes.

To make chocolate coffee cake instead of peanut butter, leave out peanut butter and instead mix ½ cup semi-sweet chocolate chips with cake batter after beating it. Then add ¼ cup semisweet chocolate chips to topping ingredients in place of peanut butter.

Francie's Favorite Coffee Cake

1½ CUPS FLOUR

¾ CUP SUGAR

2½ TEASPOONS BAKING POWDER

¾ TEASPOON SALT

¼ CUP SHORTENING

¾ CUP MILK

1 EGG

TOPPING:

⅔ CUP BROWN SUGAR, PACKED

½ CUP FLOUR

1 TEASPOON CINNAMON

6 TABLESPOONS BUTTER

Blend all ingredients except those for the topping. Beat vigorously for 30 seconds. Spread in a square cake pan. Mix together topping ingredients until crumbly. Sprinkle over batter. Bake at 375° for 25 to 30 minutes. Serve warm.

Share some love from your kitchen. Surprise your coworkers with a breakfast snack. Bake up a coffee cake and place it near the coffeepot at work.

Let us not love with words or tongue but with actions and in truth.

1 JOHN 3:18

COOKIES AND BARS

A favorite quote of mine is,

"A balanced diet is a cookie in each hand."

I say a balanced diet is TWO cookies in each hand.

And knowing there's more in the cookie jar for later

brings me a great feeling of delight!

Famous Chocolate Oatmeal Nut Cookies

Everybody's favorite cookie!

2½ CUPS OATMEAL, BLENDED	½ TEASPOON SALT
1 CUP BUTTER	1 TEASPOON BAKING POWDER
1 CUP BROWN SUGAR	1 TEASPOON BAKING SODA
1 CUP SUGAR	½ CHOCOLATE BAR, GRATED
2 EGGS	1½ CUPS WALNUTS, CHOPPED
1 TEASPOON VANILLA	12 OUNCES SEMISWEET CHOCOLATE CHIPS
2 CUPS FLOUR	

Measure oatmeal and blend to a fine powder in a blender. Cream butter and both sugars. Add eggs and vanilla; mix with flour, oatmeal, salt, baking powder, and baking soda. Add grated chocolate bar, walnuts, and chocolate chips. Form into balls and place 2 inches apart on a baking sheet. Bake at 375° for 8 to 10 minutes.

Mom's Pumpkin Cookies

1 TEASPOON VANILLA	1 TEASPOON BAKING POWDER
1 CUP SUGAR	½ TEASPOON CINNAMON
1 CUP SHORTENING	½ TEASPOON SALT
1 CUP PUMPKIN	2 CUPS FLOUR
1 EGG	1 CUP WALNUTS, CHOPPED
1 TEASPOON BAKING SODA	

Mix together vanilla, sugar, shortening, and pumpkin. Beat egg and add to mixture. In a separate bowl, combine baking soda and powder, cinnamon, salt, flour, and walnuts. Add dry ingredients to pumpkin mixture; mix well. Form into balls and place on a cookie sheet. Bake at 350° for 10 to 15 minutes.

Pumpkins are useful for more than just decoration. Sometimes there just isn't anything better than eating fresh pumpkin. Wash the pumpkin thoroughly, then cut it in half. Don't remove the seeds and pulp; place the meat side down in a large cake pan. Bake in a 300° oven until you can easily pierce the skin with a fork. The time will vary with the size of your pumpkin. When cooled, drain the juices and remove the skin and seeds. Mash the pumpkin and use as you would canned pumpkin.

You're actually encouraging our readers to spend their precious free time getting their pumpkin from an actual pumpkin? I say just add a can to your grocery list, and voilà! you have pumpkin as quickly as it takes you to open the can.

Chocolate-Peanut Butter Temptations

½ CUP BUTTER

½ CUP CREAMY PEANUT BUTTER

½ CUP SUGAR

½ CUP BROWN SUGAR

1 EGG

½ TEASPOON VANILLA

½ TEASPOON SALT

1 TEASPOON BAKING SODA

1¼ CUPS FLOUR

MINIATURE PEANUT BUTTER CUPS

Cream together butter, peanut butter, sugar, and brown sugar. Add egg, vanilla, and salt to mixture; mix well. Add baking soda and flour. Form into balls, then place in ungreased miniature muffin tins. Bake at 375° for 8 to 10 minutes. Remove from oven and immediately push peanut butter cups into cookies. Cool before removing from muffin tin.

Before washing a bowl that had flour in it, first rinse it in cold water. Hot water causes flour to gel and become harder to wash away.

Oatmeal Cookies

4 CUPS QUICK COOKING OATS

2 CUPS LIGHT BROWN SUGAR

1 CUP BUTTER, MELTED

2 EGGS, BEATEN

1 TEASPOON SALT

1 TEASPOON VANILLA

½ CUP WALNUTS, CHOPPED

Combine all ingredients and refrigerate overnight. Drop by rounded teaspoon-fuls onto a greased cookie sheet. Bake at 350° for 10 minutes.

Banana Oatmeal Cookies

1½ CUPS FLOUR

1 CUP SUGAR

½ TEASPOON BAKING SODA

1 TEASPOON SALT

¼ TEASPOON GROUND NUTMEG

¾ TEASPOON GROUND CINNAMON

¾ CUP SHORTENING

1 EGG, BEATEN

1 CUP RIPE BANANAS, MASHED
(OR USE PEELED AND
SHREDDED ZUCCHINI IN
PLACE OF ½ CUP BANANA)

1¾ CUPS ROLLED OATS

½ CUP WALNUTS, CHOPPED

In a large bowl, blend the flour, sugar, baking soda, salt, nutmeg, and cinnamon. Cut in shortening until almost no lumps remain. Stir in the egg and bananas; mix well. Add oats and walnuts. Drop by teaspoonfuls onto ungreased cookie sheets. Bake at 400° for 12 to 15 minutes or until edges are browned.

Bananas won't ripen in the refrigerator. They keep best in a paper bag at room temperature. If I can't get ripe bananas used up, I mash them, divide them into 1-cup portions, and freeze them for later use.

Chocolate Sandwich Cookies

1 CUP MARGARINE	4 CUPS FLOUR
2 CUPS SUGAR	1 TEASPOON BAKING POWDER
2 EGGS	3 TEASPOONS BAKING SODA
1 TEASPOON VANILLA	1 TEASPOON SALT
2 CUPS MILK	1 CUP COCOA

Cream margarine and sugar; add eggs, vanilla, and milk. Blend in dry ingredients. Drop by teaspoonfuls onto a greased cookie sheet. Bake at 350° for 12 minutes.

FILLING:

1 CUP MARGARINE	2 TEASPOONS VANILLA
4 CUPS POWDERED SUGAR	MILK, AS NEEDED
2 CUPS MARSHMALLOW CREAM	

When cookies are cool, mix together filling ingredients, adding enough milk so icing can be spread between cookies.

Lord, thank You for my children. May I be reminded that each meal prepared, every kitchen cleanup, each trip to the grocery store are acts of love I may pass along to my family. Amen.

Soft Batch Cookies

1 CUP SUGAR

1 CUP BROWN SUGAR

½ CUP BUTTER, SOFTENED

2 EGGS

3 CUPS FLOUR

1½ TEASPOONS BAKING SODA

1 TEASPOON SALT

2 CUPS CHOCOLATE CHIPS

Mix all ingredients together, stirring in chocolate chips last. If dough is too dry, add a small amount of water. Roll into balls and place on a cookie sheet. Bake at 350° for 10 to 12 minutes.

Raisin-Filled Cookies

2 CUPS SUGAR

1 CUP BUTTER

2 EGGS

1 CUP MILK

1 TEASPOON VANILLA

4 TEASPOONS BAKING POWDER

2 TEASPOONS BAKING SODA

5 CUPS FLOUR

Mix cookie ingredients and roll out dough. Cut out 2-inch circles.

Filling:

3 CUPS RAISINS

2 CUPS WATER

2 CUPS SUGAR

4 TABLESPOONS CORNSTARCH

Stir together filling ingredients in a large saucepan. Bring to a boil on stovetop; reduce heat and simmer until mixture thickens. Place a few scoops of filling mixture on each cookie then top with remaining cookie dough. Press edges to seal. Bake at 400° for 15 minutes or until golden.

*While these cookies aren't the easiest to make,
even I take the time to bake them.
Once you take a bite,
you'll see that the result is
definitely worth the effort.*

Lemon Cookies

1 CUP BUTTER, SOFTENED

1 CUP SUGAR

2 EGGS

2 TEASPOONS LEMON EXTRACT

3 CUPS FLOUR

½ TEASPOON BAKING SODA

1 TEASPOON SALT

Mix butter, sugar, eggs, and lemon extract. Add flour, baking soda, and salt. Place by teaspoonfuls onto an ungreased cookie sheet. Bake at 400° for 8 to 10 minutes. Let cool.

ICING:

2 CUPS POWDERED SUGAR

4 TABLESPOONS BUTTER

2 TEASPOONS LEMON EXTRACT

WATER, AS NEEDED

Mix together icing ingredients with just enough water to make a paste. Spread onto cookies.

Cake Mix Cookies

Here is a time-saver that tastes great!

1 BOX CAKE MIX (DEVIL'S FOOD,
CARAMEL, SPICE, OR
STRAWBERRY)
2 EGGS

⅓ CUP OIL
NUTS (OPTIONAL)
BAKING CHIPS (OPTIONAL)

Mix all ingredients in a bowl. Drop by teaspoonfuls onto a cookie sheet. Bake at 375° for 8 to 12 minutes.

TASTY OPTIONS FROM MARTHA'S KITCHEN:

1. Devil's food with white chocolate chips.

2. Caramel with semisweet chocolate chips and nuts.

3. Spice with nuts.

4. Strawberry dipped in powdered sugar after baking.

Oh, Martha, you're such a wonder-worker in the kitchen! Who would have believed you could do all that with one measly little cookie recipe?

Chocolate Cookies

1½ CUPS SUGAR

½ CUP SHORTENING

3 EGGS

2 CUPS FLOUR

½ TEASPOON BAKING SODA

½ TEASPOON SALT

½ CUP COCOA

POWDERED SUGAR

In a large mixing bowl, cream sugar and shortening. Add eggs then sift in dry ingredients. Chill for approximately 30 minutes. Roll in powdered sugar. Bake at 350° for 8 to 10 minutes.

When I want to freeze cookies that are frosted, I place the cookies, uncovered, on a baking sheet in the freezer for a few hours. Then when I individually wrap the cookies in plastic wrap or stack the cookies in a container, I don't have to worry about the frosting sticking. When ready to use, simply remove the cookies from their container before they thaw.

Frosted Drop Cookies

½ CUP SHORTENING

1½ CUPS BROWN SUGAR

1 TEASPOON VANILLA

2 EGGS

2½ CUPS FLOUR

1 TEASPOON BAKING SODA

1½ TEASPOONS BAKING POWDER

½ TEASPOON SALT

1 CUP SOUR CREAM

½ CUP WALNUTS, CHOPPED

BUTTER ICING

(RECIPE FOLLOWS)

Thoroughly cream shortening, brown sugar, and vanilla. Beat in eggs. Sift together dry ingredients; blend in alternately with sour cream. Stir in nuts. Drop by teaspoonfuls onto a greased cookie sheet. Bake at 350° for 10 to 12 minutes. Frost with Butter Icing.

Butter Icing

6 TABLESPOONS BUTTER

2 CUPS POWDERED SUGAR

1 TEASPOON VANILLA

HOT WATER

Heat butter until golden brown. Remove from heat and beat in powdered sugar and vanilla. Add enough hot water until mixture is the right consistency for spreading.

Grandma's Sugar Cookies

An old-fashioned recipe with great reliable taste—lard is the secret.

3 EGGS, BEATEN

2 TEASPOONS VANILLA

2 CUPS SUGAR

1 CUP LARD OR SHORTENING

½ TEASPOON BAKING SODA

1 CUP MILK

7 CUPS FLOUR

4 TEASPOONS BAKING POWDER

Mix eggs, vanilla, sugar, and lard until smooth. Blend baking soda and milk together before adding to the mixture. Sift together flour and baking powder then slowly add to the mixture until dough is the right texture for handling. Roll dough out on a lightly floured surface and cut into shapes with cookie cutters. Bake at 350° for 10 minutes.

Maple Nut Drop Cookies

1 CUP BROWN SUGAR

1 CUP BUTTER-FLAVORED SHORTENING

2 LARGE EGGS

2½ CUPS FLOUR

½ TEASPOON BAKING SODA

½ TEASPOON SALT

2½ TEASPOONS MAPLE FLAVORING

½ TEASPOON VANILLA

2 CUPS WALNUTS, CHOPPED

Cream brown sugar and shortening. Beat in eggs. Add sifted dry ingredients. Stir in maple flavoring and vanilla; add nuts. Drop by teaspoonfuls onto a greased cookie sheet. Bake at 350° for 10 to 12 minutes.

To punch up the flavor, create a maple glaze to drizzle over the tops of these cookies while they are still warm. Just combine 1½ cups powdered sugar, 1 tablespoon softened butter, ½ teaspoon maple flavoring, and enough cream or milk to make glaze the right consistency for spreading. Beat until smooth.

Monster Cookies

A monstrous mouthful.

3 EGGS

1½ CUPS BROWN SUGAR, PACKED

1 CUP SUGAR

1 TEASPOON VANILLA

1 TEASPOON CORN SYRUP

2 TEASPOONS BAKING SODA

½ CUP BUTTER

1½ CUPS PEANUT BUTTER

4½ CUPS ROLLED OATS

1 CUP SEMISWEET CHOCOLATE CHIPS

1 CUP CANDY-COATED CHOCOLATE PIECES

In a large bowl, beat the eggs. Add the remaining ingredients in order, mixing well. Use an ice cream scoop to place dough onto an ungreased cookie sheet. Bake at 350° for 12 to 15 minutes.

No-Bake Cookies

2 CUPS SUGAR

¼ CUP COCOA

¼ CUP BUTTER

½ CUP MILK

½ CUP PEANUT BUTTER

1 TEASPOON VANILLA

2½ CUPS OATMEAL

½ CUP COCONUT

In a large saucepan, boil sugar, cocoa, butter, and milk for 1 minute. Remove from heat and stir in peanut butter, vanilla, oatmeal, and coconut. Drop by teaspoonfuls onto waxed paper. Allow to cool thoroughly.

On rainy days, these cookies may take longer to set.

Snickerdoodles

1 CUP SHORTENING OR BUTTER	**3 CUPS FLOUR**
1½ CUPS SUGAR	**2 TEASPOONS CREAM OF TARTAR**
2 EGGS	**1 TEASPOON BAKING SODA**
½ TEASPOON BUTTER FLAVORING	**¼ TEASPOON SALT (OPTIONAL)**
1 TEASPOON VANILLA OR LEMON FLAVORING	**2 TEASPOONS CINNAMON**
	2 TABLESPOONS SUGAR

In a large mixing bowl, cream shortening and 1½ cups sugar. Blend in eggs and flavorings. In a separate bowl, sift flour, cream of tartar, baking soda, and salt. Stir dry mixture into sugar mixture. Form dough into balls. Blend cinnamon with 2 tablespoons sugar. Roll dough balls in the cinnamon-sugar mixture. Bake at 400° for 10 minutes on an ungreased cookie sheet. Do not overbake. Cookies should be chewy in the center.

Chocolate Mint Bars

1 CUP BUTTER

4 SQUARES UNSWEETENED
   CHOCOLATE

2 CUPS SUGAR

1 CUP FLOUR

1 TEASPOON VANILLA EXTRACT

½ TEASPOON SALT

4 EGGS

1 CUP WALNUTS, COARSELY
   CHOPPED

¾ CUP POWDERED SUGAR

1 TABLESPOON WATER

¼ TEASPOON PEPPERMINT
   EXTRACT

GREEN FOOD COLORING

In a small saucepan, melt butter and chocolate over low heat; stir often. Pour mixture into a large mixing bowl; add sugar, flour, vanilla, salt, and eggs. With mixer on low speed, beat ingredients until blended. Stir in walnuts. Pour chocolate mixture into a greased cake pan. Bake at 350° for 35 minutes or until a toothpick inserted in center comes out clean. Leave bars in the pan to cool. In a small mixing bowl, use a spoon to mix powdered sugar, water, and peppermint extract until icing is smooth. Stir in a few drops of green food coloring. Drizzle over cooled chocolate bars. After icing hardens, cut into bars of desired size. Cover and refrigerate.

Messy mixer beaters can easily be rinsed clean if you leave them on the mixer and run them in a bowl of hot water for approximately 1 minute.

Quick-N-Easy Cereal Bars

½ CUP MARGARINE

1 BAG LARGE MARSHMALLOWS

½ CUP CREAMY PEANUT BUTTER

½ CUP RAISINS

4 CUPS TOASTED OATS CEREAL

Melt margarine over low heat in a deep saucepan. Stir in marshmallows until smooth and creamy. Mix in peanut butter. Remove from heat and add raisins and cereal, stirring until evenly coated. With buttered hands, press mixture into a 9 x 13-inch cake pan. Cool; cut into bars.

Pumpkin Bars

2 CUPS FLOUR	4 EGGS, BEATEN
2 TEASPOONS BAKING SODA	2 CUPS SUGAR
2 TEASPOONS CINNAMON	1 CUP SALAD OIL
½ TEASPOON SALT	2 CUPS PUMPKIN

Combine flour, baking soda, cinnamon, and salt; set aside. Mix eggs and sugar; beat and add flour mixture, salad oil, and pumpkin. Beat into a batter. Pour batter into a rectangular, ungreased baking pan. Bake at 350° for 30 to 40 minutes.

ICING:

1 CUP MARGARINE	4 CUPS POWDERED SUGAR
2 (8 OUNCE) PACKAGES CREAM CHEESE	4 TEASPOONS VANILLA

Cream margarine and cream cheese together. Stir in powdered sugar and vanilla; beat well. Ice bars when cooled slightly.

MISCELLANEOUS DESSERTS

The proof of the pudding is in the eating.

MIGUEL DE CERVANTES (1547–1616), Spanish author

French Cherry Delight

1 POUND GRAHAM CRACKERS, CRUSHED

¾ CUP BUTTER, MELTED

2 TABLESPOONS SUGAR

1½ CUPS POWDERED SUGAR

1 (8 OUNCE) PACKAGE CREAM CHEESE, SOFTENED

3 CUPS WHIPPED TOPPING

2 CANS CHERRY PIE FILLING

Mix cracker crumbs, butter, and sugar together; press into the bottom of a 9 x 13-inch pan. Bake at 350° for 8 minutes. Allow to cool. Mix powdered sugar with cream cheese then blend in whipped topping. Spread over crust and top with cherry pie filling. Sprinkle tablespoonfuls of additional graham cracker crumbs on top for garnish.

I've gotten into the habit of buying crushed graham crackers, but when I need to, I put whole crackers in a large plastic bag and use a rolling pin to crush the crackers to a fine dust.

Jan's
Blackberry-Pineapple Delight

1 CAN BLACKBERRY PIE FILLING

1 CAN CRUSHED PINEAPPLE

1 YELLOW CAKE MIX

¼ TEASPOON BUTTER

PECANS, CRUSHED

Mix together pie filling and pineapple. Pour into an ungreased 9 x 13-inch cake
pan. Sprinkle yellow cake mix over top. Cut butter into thin slices and place over
top of cake mix, then sprinkle with crushed pecans as desired. Bake at 350° for
45 minutes. Refrigerate when cool.

Strawberry Trifle

1 ANGEL FOOD CAKE, CUBED

1 (3 OUNCE) PACKAGE INSTANT VANILLA PUDDING

1 CUP COLD MILK

1 PINT VANILLA ICE CREAM, SLIGHTLY MELTED

1 (3 OUNCE) PACKAGE STRAWBERRY GELATIN

1 CUP BOILING WATER

1 (10 OUNCE) PACKAGE FROZEN STRAWBERRIES, SLIGHTLY THAWED

In a square glass baking dish, place cubed angel food cake. In a separate bowl, place dry pudding mix, milk, and ice cream; beat until smooth then pour over cake. Dissolve gelatin in boiling water; add strawberries and cool slightly then spoon over pudding layer. Cover and refrigerate overnight.

Fresh Fruit Trifle

A low-fat dessert!

1 FAT-FREE POUND CAKE OR 1 ANGEL FOOD CAKE

⅓ CUP SUGAR-FREE STRAWBERRY JAM

4 CUPS MIXED FRESH FRUIT

(STRAWBERRIES, KIWI, BANANAS, PEACHES, BLUEBERRIES—

OR ANY COMBINATION OF YOUR FAVORITE FRUITS)

6 CUPS VANILLA PUDDING (MADE WITH SKIM MILK)

Slice cake into ¾-inch slices and spread each slice with jam on one side only. Arrange half of cake slices in the bottom of a serving bowl. Top with half the fruit then half the pudding. Repeat cake, fruit, and pudding layers.

TOPPING:

1 CUP LIGHT WHIPPED TOPPING   **1 CUP NONFAT VANILLA YOGURT**

1 CUP MIXED FRESH FRUIT (OPTIONAL)

Place whipped topping in a small bowl and fold yogurt into topping. Swirl mixture over top of the trifle and garnish with fresh fruit, if desired. Cover and chill for 2 hours before serving.

If you use bananas in this dessert, dip them in lemon juice to keep them from turning brown.

Fresh Peach Cobbler

BATTER:

½ CUP SUGAR

1 CUP FLOUR

PINCH SALT

½ TEASPOON BAKING POWDER

½ CUP BUTTER, MELTED

½ CUP MILK

Beat together batter ingredients and place in a square baking pan.

FRUIT TOPPING:

2 CUPS FRESH PEACHES, SLICED

1 CUP HOT WATER

1 CUP SUGAR

PINCH SALT

1 TEASPOON VANILLA

Mix fruit topping ingredients and pour over batter. Bake at 350° for 1 hour.

Strawberry Surprise

BOTTOM LAYER:

2 CUPS PRETZEL STICKS,
BROKEN INTO PIECES

¾ CUP MELTED BUTTER

1½ TABLESPOONS SUGAR

MIDDLE LAYER:

1 LARGE BOX STRAWBERRY
GELATIN

2 CUPS BOILING WATER

1½ CUPS COLD WATER

10 OUNCES FROZEN
STRAWBERRIES

TOP LAYER:

1 (8 OUNCE) PACKAGE CREAM
CHEESE

1 CUP SUGAR

1 (8 OUNCE) TUB WHIPPED
TOPPING

Mix together bottom layer ingredients. Place in bottom of a 9 x 13-inch cake pan and bake at 400° for 8 minutes. Set aside to cool. Mix together strawberry gelatin, boiling water, and cold water; then add frozen strawberries. Let cool; refrigerate until partially gelled. Spread over bottom layer. Mix together top layer ingredients and spoon over bottom two layers. Refrigerate until firm.

Cookie Delight

½ CUP MARGARINE, SOFTENED

1 CUP POWDERED SUGAR

1 (8 OUNCE) PACKAGE CREAM CHEESE, SOFTENED

2 SMALL BOXES INSTANT VANILLA PUDDING

3 CUPS MILK

1 TEASPOON VANILLA

1 (8 OUNCE) TUB WHIPPED TOPPING

1 LARGE PACKAGE CHOCOLATE SANDWICH COOKIES

Mix together margarine, powdered sugar, and cream cheese. In a separate bowl, combine pudding mix, milk, and vanilla; let set 3 to 5 minutes. Fold cream cheese and pudding mixtures together, then fold in whipped topping. Crush cookies. Layer half of cookie pieces in bottom of a 9 x 13-inch cake pan, then filling mixture, then crushed cookies on top. Chill for 1 hour before serving.

Butterscotch Dessert

PUDDING:

2 TABLESPOONS FLOUR

2 TABLESPOONS CORNSTARCH

½ CUP SUGAR

2 EGG YOLKS

1 CUP MILK (2% OR WHOLE)

½ CUP BUTTER (REAL BUTTER ONLY)

1 CUP BROWN SUGAR

1½ CUPS WATER

Combine flour, cornstarch, sugar, egg yolks, and milk. Set aside. Melt butter over low heat. Add brown sugar. Bring to a boil, stirring constantly. Add water and bring to a boil again. Stir flour mixture into hot mixture. Stir and cook until mixture thickens—make sure it doesn't scald. It should be the consistency of gravy when done. Cool completely in the refrigerator overnight.

CRUST:

1 BOX (3 PACKAGES) GRAHAM CRACKERS, CRUSHED

2 TABLESPOONS SUGAR

½ CUP BUTTER, MELTED

1 (8 OUNCE) TUB WHIPPED TOPPING

Mix graham cracker crumbs and sugar. Add melted butter, mixing until crumbs can be packed together. Press into a 9 x 13-inch pan. Spoon pudding over crust. Spread whipped topping over all. Sprinkle leftover graham cracker crumbs on top.

Baked Custard

4 EGGS

½ CUP SUGAR

2½ CUPS MILK

½ TEASPOON SALT

1 TEASPOON VANILLA

SPRINKLE OF NUTMEG

Mix all ingredients but the nutmeg together in a mixing bowl. Pour into a 1-quart baking dish. Sprinkle with nutmeg. Set dish in a pan of water and bake at 450° for 10 minutes, then at 350° for 25 minutes, or until it tests solid in the middle with a knife. Don't overbake or the custard will be watery.

This mixture will also fill a 9-inch unbaked piecrust.

Brownie Pudding

1 CUP FLOUR, SIFTED	1 TEASPOON VANILLA
¾ CUP SUGAR	½ CUP SEMISWEET CHOCOLATE CHIPS
2 TABLESPOONS COCOA	¾ CUP NUTS, CHOPPED
2 TEASPOONS BAKING POWDER	¾ CUP BROWN SUGAR
½ TEASPOON SALT	¼ CUP COCOA
½ CUP MILK	1¾ CUPS HOT WATER
2 TABLESPOONS VEGETABLE OIL	ICE CREAM

Sift together flour, sugar, 2 tablespoons cocoa, baking powder, and salt. Add milk, vegetable oil, and vanilla. Beat until smooth then add chocolate chips and nuts. Pour into a greased 8 x 8-inch pan. Mix brown sugar and cocoa; sprinkle over batter. Pour hot water over all. Bake at 350° for 45 minutes. Serve warm with ice cream.

Raisin Pudding

1 CUP RAISINS	**⅔ CUP SUGAR**
⅔ CUP BROWN SUGAR	**½ CUP MILK**
2 TABLESPOONS BUTTER, DIVIDED	**2 TEASPOONS BAKING POWDER**
3 CUPS COLD WATER	**FLOUR**

In a large saucepan, combine raisins, brown sugar, and 1 tablespoon butter. Boil for ten minutes. Add remaining ingredients with enough flour to make a stiff dough. Bake at 350° for 20 minutes or until nicely browned and firm.

Ozark Pudding

2 EGGS	**1 TEASPOON VANILLA**
1 TEASPOON BAKING POWDER	**2 CUPS APPLES, DICED**
1½ CUPS SUGAR	**1 CUP NUTS, CHOPPED**
½ CUP FLOUR	**WHIPPED TOPPING OR ICE CREAM**
1 TEASPOON SALT	

Beat eggs; add dry ingredients then vanilla. Fold in apples and nuts. Spread in a greased 8-inch square pan. Bake at 375° for 50 to 60 minutes. Serve warm with whipped topping or ice cream.

Pistachio Pudding Dessert

¾ CUP BUTTER, SOFTENED

1½ CUPS FLOUR

¾ CUP WALNUTS, CHOPPED

1 (8 OUNCE) PACKAGE CREAM CHEESE, SOFTENED

1 (8 OUNCE) TUB WHIPPED TOPPING, DIVIDED

1¼ CUPS POWDERED SUGAR

2 SMALL BOXES INSTANT PISTACHIO PUDDING

3 CUPS MILK

Mix butter, flour, and walnuts. Press into a 9 x 13-inch pan and bake at 350° for 15 minutes. Cool. Blend cream cheese, 1 cup whipped topping, and powdered sugar. Spread over crust. Mix pudding with milk and pour over cream cheese mixture. Refrigerate for at least 1 hour. Cover with remaining whipped topping and 1 tablespoon of additional chopped nuts.

Yellow Pudding

3 CUPS MILK, SCALDED AND DIVIDED

¼ CUP SUGAR

3 TABLESPOONS CORNSTARCH

DASH SALT

3 EGG YOLKS, BEATEN

¾ TEASPOON VANILLA

NUTMEG

Heat milk until hot but not boiling. Combine sugar, cornstarch, and salt; add to egg yolks. Add ¼ cup of the hot milk then add egg mixture to rest of hot milk. Stir constantly over medium heat until mixture thickens. Remove from heat and add vanilla. Pour into individual bowls and sprinkle each serving lightly with nutmeg.

Homemade Ice Cream

4 TO 6 EGGS, BEATEN UNTIL LIGHT
IN COLOR

1½ CUPS SUGAR

1 CAN EVAPORATED MILK (OR USE
SWEETENED CONDENSED MILK
AND REDUCE SUGAR TO 1 CUP)

2 SMALL PACKAGES INSTANT
VANILLA PUDDING

½ PINT HEAVY WHIPPING CREAM

1½ TEASPOONS VANILLA

1 TO 2 QUARTS MILK

Mix all ingredients together except the milk and pour into an ice cream freezer.

Fill to freezer's line with milk. Freeze according to freezer instructions.

Pumpkin Dessert

¾ CUP SUGAR

½ TEASPOON SALT

1 TEASPOON CINNAMON

½ TEASPOON GINGER

¼ TEASPOON GROUND CLOVES

2 LARGE EGGS, BEATEN

1 (15 OUNCE) CAN PUMPKIN PUREE

¼ CUP BISCUIT BAKING MIX

1 (12 OUNCE) CAN EVAPORATED
   MILK

WHIPPED TOPPING OR ICE CREAM

In a large mixing bowl, mix sugar, salt, cinnamon, ginger, and cloves. Add eggs to sugar mixture then blend in pumpkin. Dissolve the baking mix in a bit of the milk, then add to the pumpkin mixture. Gradually stir in the milk. Pour into a greased 8 x 8-inch baking dish. Sprinkle additional cinnamon lightly over the top. Bake at 425° for 15 minutes. Reduce heat to 350°, and bake for 40 to 50 additional minutes or until a knife inserted in the center comes out clean. Serve with whipped topping or ice cream.

For a quick way to blend these ingredients, place all ingredients, starting with milk, in the blender. Blend well. Place your prepared pan on the oven rack and pour batter from the blender directly into the pan.

Pumpkin Roll

3 EGGS

1 CUP SUGAR

²⁄₃ CUP PUMPKIN PUREE

1 TEASPOON LEMON JUICE

²⁄₃ CUP FLOUR

1 TEASPOON BAKING POWDER

2 TEASPOONS CINNAMON

1 TEASPOON GINGER

½ TEASPOON NUTMEG

½ TEASPOON SALT

1 CUP PECANS OR WALNUTS,
   CHOPPED (OPTIONAL)

1 CUP POWDERED SUGAR

1 (8 OUNCE) PACKAGE CREAM
   CHEESE, SOFTENED

4 TABLESPOONS BUTTER

½ TEASPOON VANILLA

Beat eggs with mixer on high speed for 5 minutes; gradually add sugar. Stir in pumpkin and lemon juice. In a separate bowl, sift together flour, baking powder, cinnamon, ginger, nutmeg, and salt. Add to egg mixture. Fold in pumpkin mixture. Grease and flour a jelly roll pan; spread batter in it. Top with nuts and bake at 375° for 15 minutes. Turn out cake onto a towel that has been dusted with powdered sugar. Starting at the narrow end, roll the towel and cake together; allow to cool while preparing filling. Combine powdered sugar, cream cheese, butter, and vanilla; beat until smooth. Unroll cooled cake and spread with filling. Separate towel from cake and roll cake. Cover in plastic wrap and chill. Dust with additional powdered sugar before serving.

Orange Dessert Salad

3 CUPS WATER

1 SMALL PACKAGE ORANGE GELATIN

1 SMALL PACKAGE INSTANT VANILLA PUDDING MIX

1 SMALL PACKAGE TAPIOCA PUDDING MIX

1 (15 OUNCE) CAN MANDARIN ORANGES, DRAINED

1 (8 OUNCE) CAN CRUSHED PINEAPPLE, DRAINED

1 (8 OUNCE) TUB WHIPPED TOPPING

In a large pan, boil water, then use a whisk to stir in gelatin and pudding mixes. Return to a boil while stirring for 1 minute. Remove from stove and cool completely. Fold in the fruit and whipped topping. Transfer to a container and refrigerate for 2 hours.

Pistachio Dessert Salad

1 SMALL PACKAGE INSTANT PISTACHIO PUDDING

1 (20 OUNCE) CAN CRUSHED PINEAPPLE

½ (10 OUNCE) PACKAGE MINI MARSHMALLOWS

1 (8 OUNCE) TUB WHIPPED TOPPING

Place pineapple in bottom of a large mixing bowl. Add pudding mix and blend well. Fold in marshmallows and whipped topping. Place in a serving bowl and refrigerate until firm.

Fruit Pizza

1 (8 OUNCE) PACKAGE REFRIGERATED CRESENT ROLL DOUGH
¾ CUP SUGAR
1 (8 OUNCE) PACKAGE CREAM CHEESE
1 (8 OUNCE) TUB WHIPPED TOPPING, DIVIDED
FRUIT (BANANAS, STRAWBERRIES, PEACHES,
BLUEBERRIES, PINEAPPLE, KIWI, ETC.)

Pat dough out on an ungreased round pizza pan and bake at 375° for 7 to 9 minutes or until lightly brown. Cream sugar and cream cheese; beat in 1 cup whipped topping. Add more whipped topping until mixture is spreadable. Spread over cooled crust. Place bite-sized fruit on top, overlapping in eye-catching rows. Prepare glaze for top.

GLAZE:
½ CUP SUGAR
1 TABLESPOON CORNSTARCH
½ CUP ORANGE OR PINEAPPLE JUICE
2 TABLESPOONS LEMON JUICE
¼ CUP WATER
½ TEASPOON GRATED ORANGE PEEL

Mix all ingredients together in a saucepan. Bring to a boil, stirring until mixture thickens. Let glaze cool for 1 minute then pour over pizza. Be careful not to let glaze run off the edges. Slice in thick wedges to serve.

Rhubarb Crisp

¾ **CUP SUGAR**

2 **TABLESPOONS FLOUR**

¼ **TEASPOON SALT**

4 **CUPS RHUBARB, CUT INTO**

    1-**INCH PIECES**

1 **CUP QUICK OATS**

½ **CUP BROWN SUGAR**

½ **TEASPOON CINNAMON**

¼ **CUP BUTTER, MELTED**

WHIPPED TOPPING OR ICE CREAM

Blend sugar, flour, and salt. Add rhubarb and toss lightly to mix. Place in an ungreased 8-inch square baking dish. In a mixing bowl, mix oats, brown sugar, cinnamon, and butter. Batter will be crumbly; sprinkle over the rhubarb. Bake at 350° for 35 to 45 minutes until rhubarb is tender and topping is browned. Serve warm with whipped topping or ice cream.

If you're tight on time and company will be arriving before you're able to clean up the kitchen, hide your dirty pots and pans in the dishwasher. Your guests will be shocked that you had time to prepare a delicious meal and clean up—all in a few hours' time! Then after everyone has eaten, you can place dirty plates, cups, and silverware inside, as well, and you can have a machine washing the dishes for you while you enjoy your company! Don't you just love it?

Oh, Mary, what am I ever going to do with you? I'd NEVER use a dishwasher—period! After you remove your "clean" dishes from that contraption, do you really believe they're spotless—free from food particles and germs? As far as I'm concerned, there's nothing like a good old-fashioned hand scrubbing in a sink full of sudsy hot water to get your dishes clean.

Tasty Cooked Apples

2 APPLES, PARED, CORED, AND SLICED

2 TABLESPOONS RAISINS

1 PEAR, PARED, CORED, AND SLICED

2 TABLESPOONS BROWN SUGAR

½ CUP APPLE JUICE

2 TEASPOONS LEMON JUICE

¼ TEASPOON CINNAMON

WALNUTS, CHOPPED (OPTIONAL)

Place all ingredients in a medium saucepan and bring to a boil. Simmer until fruit is soft.

*"Therefore I tell you,
do not worry about your life,
what you will eat or drink."*

MATTHEW 6:25

Tortilla Dessert Cups

3 TABLESPOONS SUGAR

2 TEASPOONS CINNAMON

10 (6 INCH) FLOUR TORTILLAS

1 CUP COLD MILK

1 SMALL PACKAGE VANILLA PUDDING MIX

1 (8 OUNCE) PACKAGE CREAM
CHEESE, SOFTENED

2 CUPS WHIPPED TOPPING

2 CUPS MIXED BERRIES

CUPS:

Blend sugar with cinnamon. Spray both sides of each tortilla with cooking spray then sprinkle with the cinnamon-sugar mixture. Cut each tortilla into 4 wedges (a pizza cutter works great). Place the round edge of one wedge into the bottom of a muffin cup, molding it to the sides. Place the second wedge on top to overlap the other. Bake at 350° for 10 minutes or until slightly browned and crisp. Store in an airtight container if not used immediately.

FILLING:

In a large bowl, whisk milk and pudding for 2 minutes. Add cream cheese and beat on low speed until blended. Fold in whipped topping. Refrigerate for 1 hour.

ASSEMBLY:

When ready to serve, spoon approximately 3 tablespoons of filling into each cup. Spoon berries on top and serve.

Experiment in your kitchen with these dessert cups. See how many different taste sensations you can create by trying out different fillings. I'll bet you find a new favorite!

PIES

Good apple pies are a considerable part of our domestic happiness.

JANE AUSTEN (1775–1817), English novelist

Perfect Apple Pie

1 CUP SUGAR

2 TABLESPOONS FLOUR

½ TO 1 TEASPOON GROUND CINNAMON

DASH GROUND NUTMEG

DASH SALT

8 TART APPLES, PARED, CORED, AND THINLY SLICED

2 TABLESPOONS BUTTER

2 UNBAKED (9 INCH) PIECRUSTS

Combine sugar, flour, cinnamon, nutmeg, and salt; add apples and stir. Line a 9-inch pie plate with prepared pastry. Fill with apple mixture; dot with butter. Adjust top piecrust, cutting slits in top. Seal and flute edges. Sprinkle with sugar. Bake at 400° for 50 minutes.

If you forget to place a piece of foil under your fruit pie and the juice bubbles out of the pan while baking, sprinkle some baking soda on the spill and let it bake to a crispy crust that can easily be brushed away when cooled.

Sour Cream Apple Pie

1 CUP SOUR CREAM	1 TEASPOON VANILLA
1 EGG	2½ CUPS APPLES, PEELED
¾ CUP SUGAR	AND DICED
2 TABLESPOONS FLOUR	1 UNBAKED (9 INCH) PIECRUST
¼ TEASPOON SALT	

Beat together sour cream and egg. Add sugar, flour, salt, and vanilla. Mix until smooth then stir in apples. Pour into piecrust. Bake at 400° for 20 minutes.

CRUMB TOPPING:

½ CUP BROWN SUGAR	⅓ CUP FLOUR
½ CUP BUTTER	1 TEASPOON CINNAMON

Mix crumb topping ingredients until crumbly. Remove pie from oven and spread crumb topping evenly over pie. Bake at 400° for 20 additional minutes.

Very Berry Pie

PASTRY FOR DOUBLE CRUST 9-INCH PIE

1 CUP SUGAR

¾ CUP FLOUR

5 CUPS MIXED BERRIES OF YOUR CHOICE

1 TABLESPOON LEMON JUICE

1 TABLESPOON BUTTER

Prepare desired pastry and divide in half; roll out one portion to fit bottom and up sides of a 9-inch pie plate. Trim edges evenly. Combine sugar and flour in a small bowl; add berries and lemon juice. Toss berries until completely coated. Pour berry mixture into pastry-lined pie plate. Dot berry mixture with butter. Roll remaining pastry into a 12-inch circle and place on top of pie filling. Cut slits in top crust for vent. Trim dough to ½ inch beyond pie plate then fold top of pastry under bottom pastry; seal and flute edges. Place pie on a baking sheet and bake at 375° for approximately 50 minutes.

If you choose to use frozen berries, first toss them with the sugar mixture while frozen. Allow to sit 15 to 30 minutes, until partially thawed, before transferring them to crust-lined pie plate.

I always use blueberries, raspberries, and blackberries in this pie. Have fun mixing your favorite berries to add your own personal touch to this dessert.

Super-Easy Peanut Butter Pie

³⁄₄ CUP CREAMY PEANUT BUTTER,
DIVIDED

3 TABLESPOONS BUTTER

1²⁄₃ CUPS GRAHAM CRACKER
CRUMBS

1 (4 SERVING) PACKAGE
VANILLA PUDDING MIX

3 CUPS MILK, DIVIDED

1 (4 SERVING) PACKAGE
CHOCOLATE PUDDING MIX

1 TEASPOON VANILLA

WHIPPED TOPPING

Heat ½ cup only of peanut butter and butter over low heat until smooth. Stir in graham cracker crumbs; remove from heat. After cool, press graham cracker mixture into a 9-inch pie plate. (Be sure to cover sides.) Place in refrigerator to chill. In a small saucepan, combine vanilla pudding mix and 1½ cups milk. Stir constantly, over medium-high heat, until mixture boils; then add remaining peanut butter. After smooth, spoon into chilled piecrust. Place back in refrigerator. Combine chocolate pudding mix and remaining milk and vanilla. Stir over medium-high heat until liquid reaches a full boil. Remove from heat and spoon over vanilla–peanut butter layer. Chill for at least 1 hour. Garnish with whipped topping before serving.

Oatmeal Pie

⅔ CUP OATMEAL, UNCOOKED

⅔ CUP CORN SYRUP

2 EGGS, BEATEN

⅔ CUP SUGAR

1 TEASPOON VANILLA

⅔ CUP BUTTER, MELTED

1 TEASPOON SALT

1 UNBAKED (9 INCH) PIE SHELL

¾ CUP PECANS, FINELY CHOPPED

 (OPTIONAL)

Mix all ingredients in order given. Pour into pie shell and sprinkle nuts on top.

Bake at 350° for 1 hour or until knife inserted in center comes out clean.

For extra appeal, I always add chocolate curls to my desserts—to top off pies, puddings, and cakes. To make chocolate curls, use a block of chocolate at room temperature and hold it in your hands for a while to warm it up. Once the chocolate is the proper temperature, run a vegetable peeler across the side of the bar using moderate pressure to produce curls. If you've never made chocolate curls before, you'll have to practice a few times to get it right; but once you see the end result, you'll agree that it's worth the extra work.

I say just throw a handful of chocolate chips on top and be done with it. Tastes the same anyway—looks pretty, too!

MAIN DISHES

The Star Attraction

The discovery of a new dish does more for human happiness

than the discovery of a new star.

from *The Physiology of Taste*
by JEAN-ANTHELEME BRILLAT-SAVARIN (1755–1826)

Meat Loaf

2 EGGS, BEATEN

8 TO 10 SODA CRACKERS

½ CUP MILK

2 POUNDS GROUND BEEF

1 SMALL ONION, CHOPPED FINE

½ GREEN PEPPER, CHOPPED FINE

1 TEASPOON SALT

¼ TEASPOON PEPPER

¼ TEASPOON GARLIC, MINCED

1 TEASPOON WORCESTERSHIRE
SAUCE (OPTIONAL)

¼ CUP TOMATO SAUCE OR
KETCHUP (OPTIONAL)

Place eggs in a large mixing bowl; beat. Crumble crackers into eggs and mix in milk. Allow crackers to get soggy. Add beef. Use hands to combine ingredients. Add rest of seasonings. Divide mixture into 2 small loaves and place in bottom of an 8 x 8-inch glass dish. Bake at 400° for 50 minutes. Remove from oven and immediately take loaves out of pan juices. (For burgers, shape mixture into patties. In a skillet, brown lightly on both sides. Cover skillet with lid and cook on low for 15 to 20 minutes.)

I like to get into my work, but I'd rather keep my hands out of raw meat. So when I make meat loaf, I place all my ingredients in a large resealable bag. Close the bag and mash the ingredients together. Push the meat into a log shape and roll it out of the bag into your baking dish. Be sure to throw the bag away when you're finished.

Pizza-Meat Loaf Roll

2 EGGS

½ CUP MILK

1 SLEEVE SODA CRACKERS

1 POUND GROUND BEEF

1 POUND PORK SAUSAGE

1 CUP CHEDDAR CHEESE, SHREDDED

½ CUP GREEN PEPPER, CHOPPED

½ CUP ONION, CHOPPED

⅛ TEASPOON PEPPER

½ TEASPOON SALT

½ TEASPOON GARLIC POWDER

½ TEASPOON OREGANO

1 CUP PIZZA SAUCE, DIVIDED

1 CUP MOZZARELLA CHEESE, SHREDDED

1 CUP PEPPERONI, SLICED

In a mixing bowl, beat eggs; add milk and crackers. Add meat, cheddar cheese, green pepper, onion, pepper, salt, garlic powder, and oregano. Mix well, using your hands. Place a cookie sheet top-down on counter and cover with waxed paper. Spread meat out on the pan, shaping it into a rectangle about 1 inch thick. Spread ½ cup pizza sauce over meat, sprinkle on mozzarella, and place pepperoni on top. Starting at the short end, use the waxed paper to help you start rolling up the meat jelly-roll style. Cut roll in half. Place into a baking dish with seams down. Drizzle ½ cup pizza sauce on top. Bake at 350° for 1 hour.

Before mealtime, spend a few moments with your family committing a scripture verse to heart. First one to learn the verse doesn't have to help with cleanup!

Stuffed Peppers

Tastes great served with mashed potatoes.

3 TO 4 POUNDS GROUND BEEF

2 TO 3 EGGS

1 CUP WHITE RICE, UNCOOKED

1 SMALL ONION, CHOPPED

1 CUP CHEDDAR CHEESE,
   SHREDDED

¼ TEASPOON SALT

¼ TEASPOON PEPPER

5 TO 6 LARGE GREEN PEPPERS

3 TO 4 LARGE CANS TOMATO
   SOUP

WATER

Mix ground beef, eggs, rice, cheese, salt, and pepper together; stuff into cleaned, hollowed-out green peppers. Place in a large soup pan with tomato soup and 3 to 4 soup cans full of water. Cook on stove over medium-high heat, boiling slowly for 3 hours.

When it comes to cooking, I say, "Just toss it in there!" Don't be afraid to experiment with ingredients and measurements. You never know what delicious concoction you might discover. A new family favorite might just be on the horizon!

Sunday Brunch Casserole

½ POUND SLICED BACON

½ CUP ONION, CHOPPED

½ CUP GREEN PEPPER,
  CHOPPED

12 EGGS

1 CUP MILK

16 OUNCES FROZEN HASH
  BROWNS, THAWED

1 CUP CHEDDAR CHEESE,
  SHREDDED

1 TEASPOON SALT

½ TEASPOON PEPPER

Cook bacon in a skillet until crisp. Remove bacon from pan with a slotted spoon. Crumble bacon and set aside. In bacon drippings, sauté onion and green pepper until tender; remove with a slotted spoon. Beat eggs and milk in a large bowl; stir in hash browns, cheese, salt and pepper, onion, green pepper, and bacon. Place in a greased baking pan. Bake uncovered at 350° for 35 to 45 minutes.

Egg-based foods can be hard to clean off plates and utensils. Sprinkle the dishes with some salt right after the meal. The salt reacts with the egg and makes for easier cleanup.

Mexican Casserole

1 POUND GROUND BEEF

1 SMALL ONION, CHOPPED

⅓ BAG NACHO CHIPS, CRUSHED

1 CAN KIDNEY BEANS

2 CUPS CHEDDAR CHEESE, SHREDDED AND DIVIDED

1 CAN STEWED TOMATOES

1 CAN CREAM OF CHICKEN CONDENSED SOUP

2 TEASPOONS CHILI POWDER

Brown ground beef over medium heat then add onion; drain. Layer in casserole dish in the following order: meat and onion mixture, nacho chips, kidney beans, 1 cup cheese, stewed tomatoes, cream of chicken soup mixed with chili powder and remaining cheese. Bake at 350° for 30 minutes.

Cleaning up a greasy mess doesn't have to be a chore if you use this little trick: Sprinkle a generous amount of baking soda into your pan when you are done cooking; add a bit of water and blend to form a paste. Let your pan stand while you and your family enjoy a meal together. When you are ready to wash your pan, it will clean up fast. You won't believe the shine! (This little cleaning tip also works wonders on the stovetop.)

Chicken Rice Casserole

1 LARGE ONION, CHOPPED

1 TABLESPOON MARGARINE

2 CUPS CHICKEN, SHREDDED

SALT AND PEPPER TO TASTE

½ CUP CARROTS, DICED

½ CUP CELERY, DICED

¼ CUP GREEN PEPPER, DICED

WATER

1 CUP WHITE RICE, UNCOOKED

Brown onion in margarine. Add chicken, salt and pepper, carrots, celery, and green pepper to a skillet. Cover completely with water. Cook over medium heat for 1 hour. Place rice in a casserole dish. Pour chicken mixture over rice and bake at 325° for 1 hour.

Chicken Casserole

1 WHOLE CHICKEN

1 CAN CREAM OF CHICKEN CONDENSED SOUP

1 CUP SOUR CREAM

BUTTER-FLAVORED CRACKERS

¼ CUP BUTTER

Cook chicken then remove from bone and shred. Mix with soup and sour cream until well blended. Pour into a greased casserole dish. Crush enough crackers to cover top. Melt butter and pour over crackers. Bake at 350° for 30 to 45 minutes.

Scrap "pizza night," and instead set aside one night a month—a Friday or Saturday—when everyone in the family will be home for a "fancy dinner night." Either experiment with a new dish you've been wanting to try or cook up a family favorite. Light some candles, set out the good dinnerware, use fancy napkins, and sip sparkling juice from elegant glasses.

Reuben Casserole

2 BAGS SAUERKRAUT, DRAINED

1 PINT SOUR CREAM

1 ONION, CHOPPED

2 CANS CORNED BEEF, CRUMBLED

2 POUNDS SWISS CHEESE SLICES

1 LOAF RYE BREAD, CUBED

1 CUP MARGARINE, MELTED

THOUSAND ISLAND DRESSING

In a large baking pan, layer as follows: 1 bag sauerkraut, sour cream, onion, second bag sauerkraut, corned beef, Swiss cheese slices, and rye bread cubes. Pour melted margarine over top. Cover and bake at 400° for 45 to 50 minutes. Remove cover and bake an additional 15 to 20 minutes until bread is browned. Cover again and bake an additional 30 minutes. Serve with Thousand Island dressing on the side.

Pizza Casserole

1 POUND GROUND BEEF	ITALIAN SEASONING
1 ONION, CHOPPED	GARLIC SALT
1 (28 OUNCE) CAN TOMATO PUREE	1 POUND SPAGHETTI, UNCOOKED
1 (8 OUNCE) CAN TOMATO SAUCE	2 CUPS MOZZARELLA CHEESE
1 SMALL CAN MUSHROOMS,	1 STICK PEPPERONI, THINLY SLICED
CUT INTO PIECES	

Brown beef with onion; drain grease. Add tomato puree, tomato sauce, and mushrooms. Add seasoning to taste and cook for approximately 5 minutes. Cook spaghetti according to package directions; drain. In a 9 x 13-inch casserole dish, place a layer of sauce (⅓) on the bottom; follow with a layer of half of the spaghetti; add more sauce with half of the cheese and pepperoni; place remaining spaghetti; top with sauce, cheese, and pepperoni. Cover with foil and bake at 400° for 30 minutes.

You don't need to cry over your onions. Try one of these solutions:

- *Keep them in the refrigerator. Warm onions easily release their fumes.*
- *Peel and cut the onion under running water.*
- *Don't cut off the bloom end of the onion, as that is where the fumes are stored.*

Mother's Macaroni Special

2 CUPS MACARONI, UNCOOKED

¼ POUND GROUND BEEF, BROWNED AND DRAINED

1 QUART WHOLE TOMATOES

12 SODA CRACKERS, CRUMBLED

1 MEDIUM ONION, MINCED

1 TEASPOON SALT

¼ CUP SUGAR

PEPPER TO TASTE

Cook macaroni in salt water; drain. In a large, heavy saucepan, combine macaroni, beef, tomatoes, crackers, onion, salt, sugar, and pepper. Bring to a boil, then stir well to loosen from sides and bottom of pan. Turn to very low heat; let simmer for 1½ hours.

Vicki's Tagalini

1 POUND GROUND BEEF

1 ONION, CHOPPED

1 GREEN PEPPER, CHOPPED

8 OUNCES SEASHELL MACARONI

1 CAN CREAMED CORN

1 CAN STEWED TOMATOES

½ CUP BLACK OLIVES, SLICED

2 TEASPOONS CHILI POWDER

SALT AND PEPPER TO TASTE

PROVOLONE CHEESE, SHREDDED

Brown ground beef; drain. Place in a large casserole dish. Add remaining ingredients. Mix gently. Bake at 350° for 30 minutes. Top with cheese and return to oven until bubbly.

Write out a variety of questions on individual strips of paper to place in a conversation-starter jar on the dinner table. Include questions such as: What's your favorite birthday memory? If you could travel to any place in the world, where would you go and why? and so on. Be creative! Each night, have a different family member pull out a conversation topic. You're guaranteed to liven up your family's conversation at the dinner table!

Yumzetti

2 POUNDS GROUND BEEF

¼ CUP ONION, CHOPPED

1 CAN TOMATO CONDENSED SOUP

1 (16 OUNCE) PACKAGE WIDE NOODLES, COOKED

1 CAN CREAM OF CHICKEN CONDENSED SOUP

SHREDDED CHEESE (OPTIONAL)

Brown meat and drain. Add onion and tomato soup. Cook noodles according to package directions then drain and add cream of chicken soup. In a square baking pan, layer beef mixture on bottom of pan, then noodle mixture. Sprinkle cheese on top, if desired. Bake at 350° for 30 minutes.

It is said that a watched pot never boils, but an unattended pot of pasta can easily boil over and create a cleaning challenge. Try rubbing butter around the top few inches of your pot to keep the water from boiling out.

Marzetti

1½ TEASPOONS VEGETABLE OIL,
DIVIDED

1 TEASPOON GARLIC POWDER

1 POUND GROUND BEEF

1 (12 OUNCE) CAN TOMATO PASTE

WATER

1 TEASPOON OREGANO

2 TEASPOONS SUGAR

2 TEASPOONS PARSLEY FLAKES

2 CUPS MACARONI, UNCOOKED

1 SMALL PACKAGE MOZZARELLA
CHEESE, SHREDDED

Heat 1 teaspoon of vegetable oil in a skillet on the stove; add garlic powder.

Brown meat in oil; drain. Lower heat and add tomato paste; fill empty can

with water and add to meat. Add additional can of water and stir. Sprinkle

in oregano, sugar, and parsley flakes. Stir and simmer for 20 minutes. Boil

macaroni in salted water with ½ teaspoon vegetable oil. Drain macaroni and add

to meat mixture. Add mozzarella and let melt, then stir thoroughly.

*This meal is great for leftovers,
but tomato sauce can stain your plastic
storage containers. I protect my
containers by spraying them with
cooking oil before filling them.*

Vegetable Lasagna

8 OUNCES LASAGNA NOODLES

2 EGGS, BEATEN

2 CUPS RICOTTA CHEESE

2 CUPS COTTAGE CHEESE

1½ TEASPOONS ITALIAN
  SEASONING

2 TABLESPOONS BUTTER

1 SMALL ONION, CHOPPED

1 CLOVE GARLIC, MINCED

2 CUPS MUSHROOMS, SLICED

2 TABLESPOONS FLOUR

½ TEASPOON PEPPER

1¼ CUPS MILK

2 (10 OUNCE) PACKAGES FROZEN
  CHOPPED SPINACH OR
  BROCCOLI, THAWED AND
  DRAINED

½ CUP SHREDDED CARROTS

¾ CUP GRATED PARMESAN
  CHEESE, DIVIDED

1 (8 OUNCE) PACKAGE
  MOZZARELLA CHEESE,
  SHREDDED

Cook noodles according to package instructions; drain and set aside. In a mixing bowl, blend eggs with ricotta and cottage cheeses and Italian seasoning; set aside. In a large skillet, melt butter and cook onion, garlic, and mushrooms until tender. Coat with flour and pepper. Add milk and cook to a boil, stirring constantly at least 1 minute. Remove from heat and add spinach or broccoli, carrots, and ½ cup Parmesan cheese. Grease a 3-quart rectangular baking dish. Divide noodles, cheese mixture, spinach mixture, and mozzarella into 3 portions. Start layering with noodles on the bottom and spread with cheese mixture. Top with spinach mixture and sprinkle with mozzarella. Repeat with two more layers. Sprinkle the top with ¼ cup Parmesan cheese. Bake uncovered at 350° for 35 minutes. Let stand for 10 minutes before serving.

Barbecued Spareribs

1 RACK RIBS

1 LARGE ONION, SLICED

1 LEMON, SLICED

1 CUP KETCHUP

⅓ CUP WORCESTERSHIRE SAUCE

1 TEASPOON CHILI SAUCE

1 TEASPOON SALT

2 DASHES HOT SAUCE

2 CUPS WATER

Place ribs in a shallow baking pan, meaty side up. On each individual rib, place 1 slice of onion and 1 slice of lemon. Roast at 450° for 30 minutes. Combine remaining ingredients in a medium saucepan and bring to a boil; pour over ribs. Continue baking for 45 minutes to 1 hour.

Grilled Chicken Breasts

CHICKEN BREASTS, BONELESS AND SKINLESS
ITALIAN DRESSING (OR TERIYAKI SAUCE)
PINEAPPLE SLICES (OPTIONAL)

Place chicken in a plastic zipper bag with dressing. Toss to coat with dressing.

Allow to marinate for at least 1 hour. Grill over medium to low heat for 6

minutes on each side. Serve with grilled pineapple for garnish.

Mix it up! Enjoy your family dinner in a location other than the dining room. Enjoy lasagna outside on a dark, starry night.... Savor grilled chicken under the shade tree in your backyard.... Devour sandwiches in your child's room.... The ever-changing environment will make dinnertime seem like a family adventure.

Huntington Chicken

4 CUPS CHICKEN BROTH

8 TABLESPOONS FLOUR

½ POUND CHEESE, GRATED (PREFERABLY PROCESSED OR COLBY)

2 CUPS MACARONI (MEASURED AFTER COOKING)

1 (4 TO 5 POUND) WHOLE CHICKEN, STEWED AND DEBONED

BUTTERED BREAD CRUMBS OR CRACKER CRUMBS

SALT AND PEPPER TO TASTE

Heat broth. Take 1 cup of broth and blend with flour to make a paste. Add to pan of broth to create a gravy. Stir in cheese until melted. Add macaroni and chicken. Place in a large baking dish. Cover with buttered bread crumbs or cracker crumbs. Sprinkle with salt and pepper. Bake at 350° for 20 to 30 minutes or until bubbly and browned.

You may freeze this chicken casserole without the crumb topping.

Crispy Baked Chicken

2 CANS CREAM OF CHICKEN CONDENSED SOUP

1 (8 OUNCE) CARTON SOUR CREAM

4 CHICKEN BREASTS, COOKED AND CUBED

1 SMALL BOX BUTTER-FLAVORED CRACKERS, CRUSHED

2 TEASPOONS POPPY SEEDS

½ CUP BUTTER, MELTED

Blend soup and sour cream; add chicken. Place in a casserole dish. Spread with crackers. Sprinkle poppy seeds on top. Pour melted butter over all. Bake at 350° for 30 minutes. Serve over rice, potatoes, toast, or biscuits.

Spanish Chicken and Rice

OLIVE OIL

4 GREEN ONIONS, DICED

1 LARGE SPANISH YELLOW
ONION, CHOPPED

2 CLOVES GARLIC, MINCED

1 CUP SPANISH GREEN OLIVES
WITH PIMENTOS, DRAINED
AND CHOPPED

1 TEASPOON CHILI POWDER

1 TEASPOON CRUSHED
RED PEPPER

2 TEASPOONS SEASONED SALT

6 BONELESS, SKINLESS CHICKEN
THIGHS, CUBED

1 (16 OUNCE) PACKAGE SPANISH
YELLOW RICE

WATER

Set electric skillet to 200–250°. Sauté onion, garlic, and olives (in enough olive oil to cover the bottom of the skillet) until onions are tender. Add seasonings and chicken. Continue to stir and cook until chicken is done through. Add rice with seasoning package and just enough water to cover the skillet's contents. Remember to thoroughly stir in seasoning. Cover and simmer until rice is desired texture, adding more water if necessary.

If your family is prone to distraction during dinnertime, I suggest the following: Turn off the TV, leave the radio off, don't answer the telephone.... Make a "no interruptions" rule at the dinner table so you can focus on just being together.

Sweet and Sour Chicken

1 POUND CHICKEN	**2 (8 OUNCE) CANS PINEAPPLE**
1 TABLESPOON VEGETABLE OIL	**CHUNKS WITH JUICE**
1 MEDIUM ONION	**3 TABLESPOONS BROWN SUGAR**
1 CLOVE GARLIC	**¼ CUP WHITE VINEGAR**
2 MEDIUM-SIZED CARROTS,	**3 TABLESPOONS SOY SAUCE**
SLICED	**3 TABLESPOONS KETCHUP**
1 MEDIUM GREEN PEPPER,	**1 TABLESPOON CORNSTARCH**
CHOPPED	**1 TEASPOON GROUND GINGER**
	WHITE RICE

Cut chicken into small chunks and brown in vegetable oil. Reduce heat to low;

add onion and pressed garlic. Cover and cook for 10 minutes. Add carrots, green

pepper, and pineapple. In a small bowl, blend brown sugar, vinegar, soy sauce,

ketchup, cornstarch, and ginger; pour over chicken mixture. Cover and simmer

for 10 minutes. Serve over cooked white rice.

*For a tasty variation of this dish,
use pork in place of chicken.*

Mexican Dinner

2 LARGE ONIONS, SLICED

1 CUP CELERY, CHOPPED

1 POUND GROUND BEEF

2 MEDIUM GREEN PEPPERS,
   FINELY SLICED

3 TABLESPOONS BUTTER

2 CUPS TOMATO JUICE

½ CUP RICE, UNCOOKED

1 TEASPOON CHILI POWDER

1 TEASPOON SALT

¼ TEASPOON PEPPER

2 TABLESPOONS SUGAR

SOUR CREAM (OPTIONAL)

In a large skillet, place onion and celery in butter; add ground beef and fry. Drain. Add remaining ingredients. Cook over medium heat for 45 minutes. Serve with sour cream if desired.

Have your family members pitch in and help at dinnertime. Everyone gets a different assignment. If you cook the meals every night, make someone else responsible for setting the table and another person in charge of cleanup. With everyone helping out, dinnertime won't seem like such a chore.

Bologna Sandwich Spread

1 POUND BOLOGNA OR HAM

½ CUP COLBY CHEESE, SHREDDED

2 HARD-BOILED EGGS

½ CUP PICKLE RELISH

½ CUP MAYONNAISE

2 TEASPOONS MUSTARD

Grind together the meat, cheese, and eggs. Mix in the relish, mayonnaise, and mustard. Chill. Serve cold on bread.

Best Barbecued Burgers

2 TABLESPOONS BUTTER

1 POUND GROUND BEEF

½ CUP ONION, CHOPPED

½ CUP CELERY, FINELY DICED

1 SMALL GREEN PEPPER,
    FINELY CHOPPED

1 CLOVE GARLIC, MINCED
    (OPTIONAL)

¼ CUP CHILI SAUCE

¼ CUP KETCHUP

1 CUP WATER

1 TEASPOON SALT

⅛ TEASPOON PEPPER

1 TABLESPOON
    WORCESTERSHIRE SAUCE

3 TABLESPOONS VINEGAR

2 TEASPOONS BROWN SUGAR

1 TEASPOON DRY MUSTARD

½ TEASPOON PAPRIKA

½ TEASPOON CHILI POWDER

1 TABLESPOON PARSLEY,
    CHOPPED

HAMBURGER BUNS

Heat butter; add beef, onion, celery, and green pepper and brown over medium-high heat. Drain. Combine remaining ingredients, except parsley, and mix well; pour over meat. Simmer for 30 minutes, stirring occasionally. Add parsley before serving. Spoon meat onto hamburger buns to serve.

I've found that hamburgers cook up faster when they're shaped a bit like a doughnut. After you form the meat into a patty, make a ¼-inch hole in the center. By the time the hamburger is cooked, the hole will have disappeared.

Rolled Sandwiches

4 LARGE FLOUR TORTILLAS
2 OUNCES CREAM CHEESE,
   SOFTENED
DIJON MUSTARD

HAM, THINLY SLICED
SALAMI, THINLY SLICED
CHEDDAR CHEESE, SHREDDED
THIN DILL PICKLE SPEARS

Spread tortillas with cream cheese and mustard. Place meat in center of each tortilla and sprinkle with cheese. Place pickle in center. Roll tortilla tightly around pickle, tucking edges in as you go and sealing edges with additional cream cheese. Wrap with plastic wrap and chill. Cut in half and serve.

Sloppy Sandwiches

1 POUND GROUND BEEF
½ SMALL ONION, CHOPPED
½ TEASPOON GARLIC, MINCED

1 CAN CREAM CONDENSED SOUP
   (CHICKEN, MUSHROOM, OR
   CELERY)

Brown beef, onion, and garlic. Add soup and simmer until thickened. Serve on bread or buns.

Joe Buns

1¼ POUNDS GROUND BEEF
1 (15 OUNCE) CAN SLOPPY JOE MIX
1 (4 OUNCE) CAN TOMATO SAUCE
12 SMALL FIRM-CRUSTED ROLLS
2 CUPS CHEDDAR CHEESE, SHREDDED

In a skillet, brown meat; drain. Add sloppy joe mix and tomato sauce; simmer for 10 to 15 minutes. Cut tops off rolls and scoop out center of each roll, leaving a crusty shell. Toss the crust from the removed centers, but add some of the soft bread to the meat mixture to absorb extra sauce; stir and simmer until bread is absorbed. Evenly distribute meat mixture into the hollowed rolls. Place rolls on a baking sheet. Sprinkle generously with cheese. Set oven on broil, and broil for 5 minutes or until cheese is melted. Serve immediately.

Let's face it. These days, it's difficult to find time for yourself. After you slide a dish into the oven, make the next half-hour "me" time. Read your Bible...pick up that new book you've been meaning to read...play a game with your kids...make a phone call to a friend you've been wanting to catch up with...talk to your husband about his day... take a catnap. However you choose to spend this time, you'll be refreshed—and looking forward to cooking your next meal!

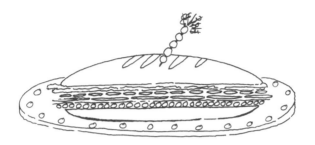

Stuffed Loaf Sandwich

1 ROUND LOAF BREAD

4 TABLESPOONS HONEY DIJON MUSTARD

9 SLICES PROVOLONE CHEESE

½ POUND TURKEY, THINLY SLICED

½ POUND HAM, THINLY SLICED

1 MEDIUM TOMATO, THINLY SLICED

Cut off the top quarter of bread; hollow out the bread, leaving a crusty wall. Spread half of mustard around on the inside of loaf. Create thin layers with cheese, meat, and tomato; repeat. Top with cheese and spread with remaining mustard. Replace top of bread. Wrap loaf with foil. Bake at 350° for 30 minutes or until heated through. Let stand for a few minutes before cutting into wedges.

Tuna Melt

4 English muffins, split (or 8 slices whole wheat bread)

2 (7 ounce) cans tuna in water, drained and flaked

¼ cup green pepper, finely chopped

1 tablespoon yellow onion, grated

6 tablespoons mayonnaise

1 teaspoon Dijon or spicy brown mustard

4 teaspoons Worcestershire sauce

¼ teaspoon pepper

8 ounces extra sharp cheddar cheese, thinly sliced

Toast English muffins and set aside. In a mixing bowl, combine tuna, green pepper, onion, mayonnaise, mustard, Worcestershire sauce, and pepper. Spread the mixture onto the 8 muffin halves and top with slices of cheese. Broil 4 inches from heat for 3 minutes or until the cheese melts and browns lightly.

Calico Beans

1 POUND GROUND BEEF	1 CAN PORK AND BEANS IN
¼ POUND BACON (OR 4 SLICES),	JUICES
CUT INTO PIECES	1 CAN KIDNEY BEANS, DRAINED
1 SMALL ONION, CHOPPED	AND RINSED
½ CUP KETCHUP	1 CAN LIMA BEANS
½ CUP BROWN SUGAR	1 CAN CUT GREEN BEANS
3 TEASPOONS PREPARED MUSTARD	1 CAN WAX BEANS
4 TEASPOONS VINEGAR	½ CUP CHEDDAR CHEESE
SALT TO TASTE	(OPTIONAL)

Sauté beef, bacon, and onion until beef is slightly browned. Drain fat. Add ketchup, brown sugar, mustard, vinegar, and salt. Pour mixture into a large casserole dish; add pork and beans and kidney beans. Pour off half the liquid from the lima, green, and wax beans; stir in with other beans. Bake uncovered at 350° for 45 to 60 minutes. You may add ½ cup of shredded cheddar cheese to the top during the last 10 minutes of baking time.

You may replace green and wax beans with butter beans and/or black beans.

Cornmeal Mush with Meat Topping

3 CUPS WATER	**1½ TEASPOONS SALT**
1 CUP CORNMEAL	**1 CUP COLD WATER**

Pour 3 cups water into a large saucepan and bring to a boil. In a small bowl, combine cornmeal, salt, and cold water until smooth. Gradually stir the cornmeal into the boiling water. Continue boiling, stirring constantly until mixture is thickened. Cover and lower heat. Cook slowly for 10 to 12 minutes. While still hot, dish into bowls and serve with meat topping.

Leftover cornmeal mush can be packed into a loaf pan and refrigerated. To use, slice and fry. Serve with maple syrup.

TOPPING:

½ POUND GROUND BEEF	**SALT**
OR SAUSAGE	**PEPPER**
½ SMALL ONION	**GARLIC POWDER (OPTIONAL)**

Brown meat and onion; drain grease. Season to taste.

Ham Loaf

3 ROLLS OR BUNS, CRUMBLED

1 TEASPOON MILK

2 TO 3 EGGS

1 POUND GROUND HAM

1 POUND GROUND PORK

½ CUP VINEGAR

½ CUP WATER

1 CUP BROWN SUGAR

1 TEASPOON MUSTARD

Moisten bread with milk; add eggs and meat. If too moist, add more bread. If too dry, add more milk. Shape into 2 loaves and place in loaf pans. Bake at 350° for 1½ hours. In a saucepan, combine vinegar, water, brown sugar, and mustard; boil and pour over meat. Baste meat with sauce while baking.

Homemade Pizza

Dough:

1 PACKAGE ACTIVE DRY YEAST

1 CUP WARM WATER

1 TEASPOON SUGAR

1 TEASPOON SALT

2 TABLESPOONS OIL

2½ CUPS FLOUR

Dissolve yeast in warm water. Stir in remaining ingredients and beat vigorously, about 20 strokes. Allow dough to rest and rise. Spread out on 2 pizza rounds.

Sauce:

½ CUP ONION, CHOPPED

1 (8 OUNCE) CAN TOMATO SAUCE

1 TEASPOON ITALIAN SEASONING

⅛ TEASPOON GARLIC POWDER

Mix sauce ingredients and spoon over dough. Top with favorites (green pepper, pepperoni, ground beef, shredded mozzarella, mushrooms, etc.). Bake at 375° for 20 to 25 minutes.

The homemade crust is what makes this an extra special family treat.

Martha, I believe you know how to make "homemade" everything. But for a great shortcut, I use a prepared pizza shell from the grocery store. As an added bonus, the kids will love to help with placing the toppings on the pizza. They'll be delighted to create their own favorite flavor combinations.

Oh, and be sure to try some of these interesting pizza toppers (if you dare!): pineapple, peanuts, artichokes, taco-type toppings, seafood... Though I wouldn't recommend using them all on the same pizza!

Pizza Wrap

1 PACKAGE HOT ROLL MIX

¾ CUP WARM WATER

1 EGG

1 POUND GROUND BEEF, BROWNED
AND DRAINED

1 (15 OUNCE) JAR SPAGHETTI SAUCE

OLIVES (OPTIONAL)

1 (4 OUNCE) CAN SLICED
MUSHROOMS, DRAINED

6 OUNCES MOZZARELLA OR
CHEDDAR CHEESE, SLICED
OR SHREDDED

In a large bowl, dissolve yeast from hot roll mix in warm water; stir in egg. Add flour mixture from mix; blend well. Toss dough onto a floured surface until no longer sticky. Roll out to a 12 x 14-inch rectangle; place on a greased cookie sheet. Combine beef, 1 cup of sauce, olives, and mushrooms; spoon filling down longest center third of dough, leaving 1½ inches at each end. Place cheese on top of filling. Fold 1½-inch edges over ends of filling; seal edges of dough. Fold ⅓ of uncovered dough completely over filling, stretching to cover. Fold remaining ⅓ of dough over filling and dough layer, stretching to cover. Pinch well to seal all edges. Flatten loaf slightly to a 5 x 12-inch rectangle. Using a sharp knife, slash top of loaf 4 to 5 times. If desired, brush with beaten egg and sprinkle with sesame seeds. Bake at 400° for 20 to 35 minutes or until deep golden brown. Cut into slices and serve with heated reserved sauce. Refrigerate leftovers.

Soy Hamburg Meal

½ POUND GROUND BEEF

2 CUPS MIXED VEGETABLES

4 CUPS COOKED RICE

1 TO 2 TABLESPOONS SOY SAUCE

Brown ground beef and drain grease. Cook vegetables according to package directions; drain. Combine beef, vegetables, rice, and soy sauce. Serve warm.

I detest cleaning up starchy water from the sides and lid of the rice pot. After I add rice to the water and turn the burner to low, I cover the pot with a folded dishtowel, then hold it in place with the pot's lid. As the rice cooks, the towel absorbs the water and cleanup is a snap.

SALADS

Not Just Lettuce

The kitchen is the great laboratory of the household. . . .

from *The Book of Household Management*
by Isabella Beeton (1836–1865)

Pasta Salad

1 POUND TWIST PASTA

8 OUNCES ITALIAN DRESSING

8 OUNCES MOZZARELLA CHEESE, CUBED

1 CUP RED ONION, CHOPPED

1 CUP GREEN PEPPER, DICED

1 CUP BLACK OLIVES

1 PACKAGE PEPPERONI

Cook pasta according to package directions; drain and rinse. Combine all ingredients; toss well to make sure pasta, cheese, vegetables, and pepperoni are coated with dressing. Chill until ready to serve.

Cheesy Bacon Cauliflower Salad

Mary's signature salad.

1 LARGE HEAD LETTUCE

1 HEAD CAULIFLOWER

½ RED ONION, CHOPPED

1 (10 OUNCE) BAG FROZEN PEAS

1 TEASPOON SUGAR

1 (16 OUNCE) JAR MAYONNAISE

2 CUPS CHEDDAR CHEESE, SHREDDED

1 POUND THIN-SLICED BACON, COOKED, DRAINED, AND CRUMBLED

6 HARD-BOILED EGGS

In a large bowl, mix lettuce, cauliflower, onion, and peas. In a separate bowl, mix sugar and mayonnaise; spread on top of salad mixture then sprinkle with cheese and bacon. Cover and refrigerate overnight. When ready to serve, chop hard-boiled eggs and add to salad.

When I'm going to cut up a whole head of lettuce, I always use this nifty tip: To get the core out, I just give the head's core a whack down on my countertop. Then I give the core a twist, and it comes right out.

Tangy Cauliflower Salad

1 CUP MAYONNAISE

⅓ CUP HONEY

1 TABLESPOON PREPARED MUSTARD

1 LARGE CAULIFLOWER HEAD BROKEN INTO FLORETS (6 CUPS)

1 CUP SEEDLESS GRAPES, HALVED

1 CUP WALNUTS, CHOPPED

Combine mayonnaise, honey, and mustard in a bowl; add cauliflower, grapes, and walnuts. Stir to coat. (Cauliflower will naturally darken after 12 to 24 hours in the dressing.)

I used to despise finding crystallized honey in my kitchen cupboard—until I learned how to reverse it. Crystallization is a natural process for honey, but it doesn't mean you have to throw it out. Place the jar of honey in a pan of warm water and stir the honey until the crystals dissolve. You can also microwave the honey for 30 seconds, stir, and repeat for another 30 seconds until the crystals have dissolved.

Taco Salad

1 POUND GROUND BEEF

1 PACKAGE TACO SEASONING

1 MEDIUM HEAD LETTUCE, CHOPPED

1 SMALL CAN KIDNEY BEANS

1 LARGE ONION, CHOPPED

4 MEDIUM TOMATOES, DICED

8 OUNCES CHEDDAR CHEESE, SHREDDED

1 PACKAGE NACHO CHIPS, CRUSHED

SALSA

SOUR CREAM

Brown ground beef; drain. Add taco seasoning. Layer salad ingredients in a bowl, starting with lettuce and ending with cheddar cheese; chill. When ready to serve, add crushed nacho chips. Serve with salsa and sour cream.

3-Bean Salad

1 CAN WAX BEANS, DRAINED

1 CAN GREEN BEANS, DRAINED

1 CAN KIDNEY BEANS, DRAINED

1 SMALL ONION, MINCED

⅓ CUP SUGAR

1 TEASPOON SALT

¼ TEASPOON PEPPER

½ CUP VINEGAR

½ CUP OIL

½ CUP WATER

2 EGGS, HARD-BOILED AND
SLICED (OPTIONAL)

Combine beans and onion in a large serving bowl. Thoroughly mix sugar, salt, pepper, vinegar, oil, and water; pour over beans. Garnish with egg slices. Allow to chill and season in refrigerator for a few hours before serving.

24-Hour Slaw

1 HEAD CABBAGE

1 SMALL ONION

1 CUP CELERY, FINELY CHOPPED

1 GREEN PEPPER, FINELY
CHOPPED

2 CUPS SUGAR

½ CUP VINEGAR

1 TEASPOON SALT

½ TEASPOON CELERY SEED

1 TEASPOON MUSTARD SEED

Shred cabbage and onion in a blender or food processor—not too fine. Place all vegetables in a large mixing bowl. Mix sugar, vinegar, and seasoning; pour over vegetables. Cover and refrigerate for 12 to 24 hours.

Cucumbers with Vinegar Dressing

¼ CUP WATER

¼ CUP SUGAR

¼ CUP VINEGAR

¼ TEASPOON SALT

DASH PEPPER

½ SMALL ONION, THINLY SLICED

4 CUPS CUCUMBERS, PEELED AND THINLY SLICED

Blend water, sugar, vinegar, salt, and pepper; add onion and cucumbers. Cover and refrigerate for at least 2 hours.

I like to use a bit of bacon in many recipes. I cook up a pound of bacon at one time until done but not crisped. When cooled and drained of fat, I cut or crumble the bacon and store it in a freezer container. It can then be quickly added to a casserole or salad.

Caramel Apple Salad

1 SMALL PACKAGE INSTANT BUTTERSCOTCH PUDDING

1 (8 OUNCE) TUB WHIPPED TOPPING

1 (10 OUNCE) CAN CRUSHED PINEAPPLE, INCLUDING JUICE

1 CUP MINIATURE MARSHMALLOWS

3 CUPS APPLES, PARED AND CUT INTO SMALL CHUNKS

Mix all ingredients together; refrigerate for 1 hour before serving.

Cinnamon Cherry Salad

1 CUP BOILING WATER

¼ CUP RED HOT CINNAMON CANDIES

1 SMALL PACKAGE CHERRY GELATIN

1 CUP COLD WATER

1 CUP APPLESAUCE

Bring water to a boil; turn to low heat and dissolve candies, stirring constantly. Stir in gelatin until dissolved. Pour into a glass dish. Add cold water and applesauce. Chill until firm.

Wilted Lettuce Salad

2 SLICES BACON, FRIED CRISP, DRAINED, AND CRUMBLED

1 TABLESPOON BACON DRIPPINGS

2 TABLESPOONS WATER

2 TABLESPOONS VINEGAR

DASH SALT

2 TO 3 TABLESPOONS SUGAR

1 TABLESPOON CORNSTARCH

LETTUCE

After cooking bacon, remove from heat and pour off all but 1 tablespoon of grease. Add water, vinegar, and salt to slightly cooled drippings; return to heat. Combine sugar and cornstarch; stir into pan mixture and cook until it thickens. Add bacon. Serve hot over lettuce.

Make meal planning a family event. One day, you choose what goes on the menu, then the rest of the week, your family members can take turns choosing the main course. Post the weekly menu on a chalkboard or Dry-Erase board in the kitchen. You'll find that everyone looks forward to suppertime…and you'll rarely hear, "What's for dinner?" The added benefit is that your grocery list will be easier to write out, and you won't be scrambling to decide what to cook for supper every evening.

Classic Potato Salad

1 CUP MAYONNAISE

2 TABLESPOONS VINEGAR

1 TEASPOON SUGAR

1½ TEASPOONS SALT

¼ TEASPOON PEPPER

4 CUPS POTATOES, BOILED AND CUBED

1 CUP CELERY, SLICED

½ CUP ONION, CHOPPED

2 HARD-BOILED EGGS, CHOPPED

Blend mayonnaise, vinegar, sugar, salt, and pepper; pour over mixture of potatoes, celery, onion, and eggs. Chill until ready to serve.

Potato Salad Pizza Style

6 TO 10 MEDIUM POTATOES, COOKED UNTIL TENDER AND CHOPPED

1 SMALL ONION, DICED

1 SMALL GREEN PEPPER, DICED

1 CUP PEPPERONI, DICED

1 CUP SHARP CHEDDAR CHEESE, SHREDDED

2 TO 3 HARD-BOILED EGGS, CHOPPED

½ TO 1 TEASPOON SALT

⅛ TEASPOON PEPPER

½ TEASPOON CELERY SALT

½ TO 1 CUP MAYONNAISE

1 CUP CATALINA SALAD DRESSING

PARMESAN CHEESE

PEPPERONI SLICES

Place potatoes, onion, green pepper, pepperoni, cheese, and egg in a large mixing bowl. Season with salt, pepper, and celery salt. Stir in just enough mayonnaise to lightly coat the vegetables. Add dressing; mix well. Place in a serving dish. Garnish with a sprinkling of Parmesan cheese, pepperoni slices, and some cheddar cheese. Refrigerate for several hours before serving.

Summer Chicken Salad

1 CUP MAYONNAISE

1 TABLESPOON DIJON MUSTARD

1½ TABLESPOONS VINEGAR

1 TEASPOON GARLIC POWDER

½ TEASPOON SALT

2 TO 3 CHICKEN BREASTS, COOKED, CUBED, AND CHILLED

8 OUNCES ROTILLA PASTA, COOKED AND RINSED IN COLD WATER

1 GREEN BELL PEPPER, CHOPPED

½ SMALL ONION

2 CUPS GRAPES, SLICED IN HALF

½ CUP SLICED ALMONDS

Blend mayonnaise, mustard, vinegar, garlic powder, and salt. Place chicken, pasta, bell pepper, onion, and grapes in a large bowl. Coat with dressing and chill for at least 1 hour. Add almonds when ready to serve.

SIDE DISHES

Potatoes and Beyond

The ambition of every good cook

must be to make something very good

with the fewest possible ingredients.

Urbain Dubois (1818–1901), European chef and author

Home-Style Baked Beans

1 (16 OUNCE) CAN PORK AND BEANS

¼ CUP ONION

½ TEASPOON MUSTARD

¼ CUP KETCHUP

2 TABLESPOONS BROWN SUGAR

4 SLICES BACON, COOKED

Place all ingredients in a baking dish and bake, covered, at 325° for 1½ hours.

Scalloped Corn

2 EGGS

2 TABLESPOONS SUGAR

2 CUPS CORN

1 CUP MILK

¼ CUP BUTTER

½ TEASPOON SALT

¼ CUP FLOUR

2 TABLESPOONS GREEN PEPPER,
CHOPPED

In a greased quart baking dish, beat eggs and blend in sugar and corn. In a separate small bowl, beat together milk, butter, salt, and flour. Combine milk mixture with corn mixture. Fold in green pepper. Bake at 350° for approximately 1 hour.

Baked Corn

1 CAN CREAM-STYLE CORN	**1 (8½ OUNCE) BOX CORN**
1 CAN WHOLE KERNEL CORN	**MUFFIN MIX**
2 EGGS	**½ CUP MARGARINE**
1 CUP SOUR CREAM	

Mix together all ingredients except margarine; place in a baking dish. Melt margarine and pour over corn mixture. Bake at 350° for 30 to 40 minutes.

Make a habit of thanking the Lord before each meal. After all, He's the one who's given us such abundance; because of His goodness, we can eat our fill and not go hungry each night. Take turns giving thanks around the dinner table. Have each member of your family participate. Prepare to be amazed at how the Lord has blessed each one of you.

I will tell of the kindnesses of the LORD,

the deeds for which he is to be praised,

according to all the LORD has done for us—

yes, the many good things he has done.

ISAIAH 63:7

Aunt Diane's Broccoli Cheese Casserole

1 MEDIUM ONION

½ CUP MARGARINE

1 CAN CREAM OF CHICKEN CONDENSED SOUP

¾ CUP MILK

½ POUND PROCESSED CHEESE, DICED

1 CUP MINUTE RICE, UNCOOKED

2 SMALL PACKAGES FROZEN CHOPPED BROCCOLI

Sauté onion in margarine. Add cream of chicken soup, milk, and cheese; stir until cheese is melted. Add rice and broccoli. Pour mixture into a baking dish and bake uncovered at 325° for 45 to 50 minutes.

Make it a priority to include your entire family around the table for dinner at least one night a week. Discuss each other's activities of the day and revel in the warmth this togetherness brings to your heart.

Joanne's Brown Rice Casserole

1¼ CUPS NATURAL LONG-GRAIN RICE

1 CAN FRENCH ONION CONDENSED SOUP

1 CAN BEEF BROTH BOUILLON

2 CANS (4 OUNCES EACH) MUSHROOMS, DRAINED

½ CUP MARGARINE

Mix all ingredients except margarine in a casserole dish. Slice margarine into

squares and place over top of casserole mixture. Cover; bake at 350° for 1 hour.

*This recipe doubles well.
Follow same baking time.*

Sweet Potatoes

2 TABLESPOONS MARGARINE

5 LARGE CANS SWEET POTATOES

FLOUR

4 SMALL CARTONS WHIPPING CREAM

BROWN SUGAR TO TASTE

Melt margarine in a skillet. Roll potatoes in flour, then brown in margarine. Place potatoes in two baking pans and dot with margarine. Sprinkle brown sugar on top to taste, then pour juice from skillet over top. Pour whipping cream over potatoes. Bake, covered, at 350° for 30 minutes.

Nutty Sweet Potato Casserole

4 EGGS, SLIGHTLY BEATEN

1 CUP BUTTER, MELTED

2 CUPS SUGAR

1 CUP FLAKED COCONUT

1 CUP EVAPORATED MILK

2 TEASPOONS BAKING POWDER

1 TEASPOON VANILLA

4 CUPS MASHED SWEET POTATOES (CANNED OR FRESH)

Mix ingredients in the order given. Pour into a large, greased, deep-dish casserole pan.

TOPPING:

1 CUP BROWN SUGAR

½ CUP FLOUR

1 CUP PECANS, CHOPPED

½ TEASPOON SALT

½ TEASPOON BAKING POWDER

¼ CUP BUTTER

Mix first 5 ingredients; spread onto potato mixture. Dot with butter. Bake at 350°, uncovered, for 1 hour. Top should be firm and crusty, and inserted knife will come out clean when casserole is done.

Baked Cheesy Potatoes

1 (2 POUND) PACKAGE FROZEN HASH BROWNS

1 CAN CREAM OF POTATO CONDENSED SOUP

1 CAN CREAM OF CELERY CONDENSED SOUP

HANDFUL OF ONIONS

1½ CUPS SOUR CREAM

SALT

PEPPER

1 CUP CHEDDAR CHEESE, SHREDDED AND DIVIDED

Place hash browns in a large baking dish. Mix potato soup, celery soup, onions, sour cream, salt, and pepper (to taste), and ½ cup cheddar cheese. Pour mixture over hash browns then sprinkle ½ cup cheddar cheese over top. Bake at 350° for 1 hour.

Have a dinner-and-a-movie night with your family. Make a simple dish, and gather everyone in the living room to enjoy dinner and watch a family-friendly movie.

Sloppy Potatoes

3 MEDIUM POTATOES, SLICED   ½ TEASPOON SALT

1 MEDIUM ONION, SLICED   ½ CUP WATER

1 TABLESPOON BUTTER

In a medium saucepan, bring all ingredients to a boil. Reduce heat to low and cook for 15 minutes, stirring occasionally.

Sherry's Steak Potatoes

8 LARGE POTATOES, UNPEELED   ½ TEASPOON PAPRIKA

⅓ CUP VEGETABLE OIL   2 TABLESPOONS FINE BREAD

¼ TEASPOON SALT   CRUMBS

2 TABLESPOONS GRATED   1 TABLESPOON GARLIC POWDER

   PARMESAN CHEESE   FRENCH ONION DIP

Cut each potato into 8 wedges. Mix all other ingredients in a large container with tight-fitting lid. Shake potatoes in mixture and place skin side down on a cookie sheet. Pour any remaining mixture over potatoes. Bake at 375° for 45 minutes. Serve with French onion dip.

Green Bean Casserole

1 CAN French-style green beans, drained

1 CAN CREAM OF MUSHROOM CONDENSED SOUP

1 CAN French-fried onion rings

Place green beans in a casserole dish. Add mushroom soup and ½ can onion rings; blend. Bake at 250° for 20 minutes. Top with remaining onion rings and bake for an additional 10 minutes.

Invite your friends over for a night of recipe sharing. Have each person bring a covered dish (preferably from different categories)—so you'll have a salad, soup, bread, side dish, a main dish, and a dessert. Enjoy the meal and conversation. Be sure to have the various recipes written out on cards beforehand, so everyone leaves with new dishes to try at home.

Squash Medley

½ MEDIUM GREEN ZUCCHINI, SLICED OR CHUNKED

½ MEDIUM GOLD ZUCCHINI, SLICED OR CHUNKED

2 TO 4 PODS OKRA, SLICED

½ SMALL ONION, CHOPPED

¼ LARGE GREEN PEPPER, CHOPPED

1 PINT CANNED TOMATOES OR 3 FRESH TOMATOES, CHOPPED

1 CHICKEN BOUILLON CUBE

½ TEASPOON GARLIC, MINCED

1 TEASPOON SUGAR

½ TEASPOON SALT

Place all ingredients in a saucepan. Bring to a boil; lower heat. Let simmer until vegetables are tender.

Roy's Favorite
Fried Green Tomatoes

VEGETABLE OIL

¾ CUP FLOUR

¼ CUP CORNMEAL

¼ TEASPOON SALT

¼ TEASPOON PEPPER

2 LARGE GREEN TOMATOES,
    SLICED MEDIUM THIN

¾ CUP MILK

Cover bottom of a frying pan with oil; heat. Blend flour, cornmeal, salt, and

pepper. Dip tomato slices in milk then coat in dry mix. Fry, turning once, until

tomatoes reach desired browned—or charred—look. Serve on bread with

butter.

Stewed Tomatoes

1 QUART CANNED TOMATOES

1 TEASPOON SALT

¼ CUP SUGAR

1 TABLESPOON BUTTER

2 TABLESPOONS FLOUR

½ CUP MILK

SODA CRACKERS OR BREAD

In a medium saucepan, cook tomatoes with salt for 15 minutes. Add sugar and butter. Slowly combine flour and milk until there are no lumps. Add floury milk to tomatoes, stirring over heat until thickened. To serve, break up crackers or bread in a serving dish and pour tomatoes over top. Stir and serve.

Two-Cheese Spinach

2 (10 OUNCE) PACKAGES FROZEN CHOPPED SPINACH

5 TABLESPOONS BUTTER, DIVIDED

1 CUP RICOTTA CHEESE OR SMALL CURD COTTAGE CHEESE

1 EGG

3 TABLESPOONS FLOUR

¼ TEASPOON SALT

⅛ TEASPOON PEPPER

⅛ TEASPOON GROUND NUTMEG

3 TABLESPOONS GRATED PARMESAN CHEESE

Place spinach in a large saucepan and cook according to package instructions.

Drain the cooked spinach through a colander or sieve, pressing out the liquid.

Melt 3 tablespoons butter in the same pot then remove from heat. Stir in

spinach, ricotta cheese, egg, flour, salt, pepper, and nutmeg. Mix thoroughly.

Place mixture in a greased 8 x 8-inch baking dish. Dot top with remaining butter

and sprinkle with Parmesan cheese. Bake uncovered at 425° for 10 minutes until

cheeses are melted.

SOUPS

Spoonfuls of Comfort

Ponder well on this point:

The pleasant hours of our life are all connected by a

more or less tangible link with some memory of the table.

CHARLES PIERRE MONSELET (1825–1888), French chef

Mom's Chili

Tastes great on chilly winter days!

2–3 POUNDS GROUND BEEF

3 LARGE CANS TOMATO CONDENSED SOUP

WATER

2 LARGE CANS KIDNEY BEANS

1 (12 OUNCE) CAN TOMATO PASTE

CHILI POWDER (AS DESIRED)

Brown ground beef; drain. In a large saucepan, mix beef with tomato soup and 3 soup cans full of water. Drain kidney beans; add to ground beef mixture. Add tomato paste (to thicken soup). Sprinkle in chili powder to desired taste. Cook over medium heat for 30 to 45 minutes.

Grandma's Potato Soup

4 CUPS POTATOES

½ CUP CARROTS, DICED

½ CUP CELERY, DICED

2 CUPS WATER

1 TEASPOON DRIED ONION

2 TABLESPOONS BUTTER

¼ CUP FLOUR

2 CUPS CHICKEN BROTH (MADE
FROM 2 CUPS BOILING WATER
AND CHICKEN SOUP BASE)

½ TEASPOON PARSLEY FLAKES

1 CUP PROCESSED CHEESE,
CUBED

Peel, quarter, and slice potatoes. Place in a large saucepan with carrots, celery, water, and dried onion. Bring to a boil, and cook for approximately 10 minutes. In a small pan, melt butter and blend in flour and chicken broth. Cook for 5 minutes, until thickened. Add broth and flour mixture to cooked potatoes. Do not drain. Add parsley and cheese; heat but do not boil. Stir to blend.

Instant mashed potatoes can be added to thicken soup. To thin, add additional chicken broth.

Cheesy Broccoli Soup

1½ CUPS WATER

1 BUNCH BROCCOLI, CHOPPED

1 LARGE STALK CELERY,
   CHOPPED

2 TABLESPOONS MARGARINE

2 TABLESPOONS FLOUR

2 CUPS WATER

½ CAN CHEDDAR CHEESE
   CONDENSED SOUP

1 TABLESPOON INSTANT CHICKEN
   BOUILLON

¼ TEASPOON SALT

⅛ TEASPOON PEPPER

½ CUP WHIPPING CREAM

In a large saucepan, bring 1½ cups water to a boil; add vegetables. Cover and cook until vegetables are tender, approximately 10 minutes. Do not drain. Run broccoli through a blender. Melt margarine in a saucepan over low heat; stir in flour. Cook until smooth and bubbly then remove from heat. Add 2 cups water. Bring to a boil, stirring constantly. Add cheese soup, broccoli mixture, bouillon, salt, and pepper. Heat to boiling; reduce heat and stir in whipping cream.

Kitchens aren't just for creating palate-pleasing meals.... Maybe even more important are some of the loveliest memories, which are created there.

Cheeseburger Soup

½ POUND GROUND BEEF

¾ CUP ONION, CHOPPED

¾ CUP CARROTS, SHREDDED

¾ CUP CELERY, DICED

1 TEASPOON BASIL

1 TEASPOON PARSLEY

4 TABLESPOONS MARGARINE,
DIVIDED

3 CUPS CHICKEN BROTH

4 CUPS POTATOES, DICED

¼ CUP FLOUR

8 OUNCES PROCESSED CHEESE,
CUBED

1½ CUPS MILK

¾ TEASPOON SALT

½ TEASPOON PEPPER

¼ CUP SOUR CREAM

Brown ground beef and drain. In a large saucepan, sauté onion, carrots, celery, basil, and parsley in 1 tablespoon margarine. Add chicken broth, potatoes, and beef; bring to a boil and reduce heat. Cover and simmer for 10 to 12 minutes, until potatoes are done. In a small skillet, stir remaining margarine and flour on low to medium heat for 3 to 5 minutes; add to soup. Boil for 2 minutes then reduce heat to low. Add cheese, milk, salt, and pepper. Continue heating until cheese melts. Remove from heat and add sour cream.

Salt is a wonderful flavor enhancer, but too much salt can spoil the whole recipe. If your soup ends up with too much salt, cut a raw potato (or turnip) into large chunks and drop them in the soup for several minutes. The potato will naturally absorb the salt and can be removed before serving.

Hearty Chicken Soup

3 PIECES CHICKEN ON THE BONE

4 CUPS WATER

2 CUPS CANNED CHICKEN BROTH

1 LARGE CARROT, SLICED

1 STALK CELERY, CHOPPED

2 TABLESPOONS ONION, CHOPPED

1 TEASPOON ROSEMARY OR ROSEMARY HERB MIX

½ TEASPOON CURRY POWDER

⅛ TEASPOON PEPPER

1 BAG FROZEN HOME-STYLE NOODLES

Boil chicken in 2 cups water for 20 minutes. Remove chicken from the pot; cool and debone. Return chicken to the pot; add rest of ingredients except noodles. Bring to a boil then add noodles. Simmer for 20 minutes.

Ribble Soup

2 LARGE POTATOES, PEELED
AND DICED

2 STALKS CELERY, FINELY
CHOPPED

1 SMALL ONION, DICED
(OR SUBSTITUTE ½ TEASPOON
ONION POWDER)

3 CUPS WATER

3 CHICKEN BOUILLON CUBES

1½ TEASPOONS SALT

¼ TEASPOON PEPPER

1 CUP FLOUR

1 LARGE EGG

½ TO 1 CUP MILK

1 TABLESPOON BUTTER

Bring vegetables to a boil in water, then add bouillon, salt, and pepper. In a small mixing bowl, blend flour and egg with a fork, cutting together until mixture is in small pieces. Add ribbles to boiling soup. Stir soup often as it cooks over low heat, until vegetables are soft and ribbles are tender. Add milk and butter. Heat through, but do not boil. Adjust amount of liquid to your liking.

To slice potatoes with ease, first heat your knife in boiling water or over a gas flame.

Nifty Substitutions

A Little of This, Plus a Pinch of That

Have you ever started to mix together ingredients for a recipe, only to find that you're missing an important item? Don't fret! Before you toss what you're preparing—and before running all the way to the grocery store—check out this list. We've found that the following substitutes work wonders when you're in a pinch.

ALLSPICE

1 teaspoon allspice = ½ teaspoon cinnamon plus ½ teaspoon ground cloves

BAKING POWDER

1 teaspoon baking powder = ¼ teaspoon baking soda plus ⅝ teaspoon cream of tartar

BUTTERMILK

1 cup buttermilk = 1 cup milk plus 1 tablespoon lemon juice or white vinegar (let stand 5 minutes before using)

BROWN SUGAR

½ cup brown sugar (firmly packed) = 1 cup white sugar or ½ cup white sugar plus 2 tablespoons molasses

CORNSTARCH (FOR THICKENING)

1 tablespoon cornstarch = 2 tablespoons all-purpose flour or 2 tablespoons granular tapioca

CORN SYRUP

1 cup corn syrup = 1 cup sugar plus ¼ cup liquid or 1 cup honey (use whatever liquid is called for in recipe)

GARLIC

1 small clove of fresh garlic = ⅛ teaspoon garlic powder

HERBS

1 tablespoon fresh-cut herbs = 1 teaspoon dried herbs

HONEY

1 cup honey = 1¼ cups sugar and ¼ cup liquid (use whatever liquid is called for in recipe)

LEMON JUICE

    1 teaspoon lemon juice = ½ teaspoon vinegar

MUSTARD

    1 teaspoon dry mustard = 1 tablespoon prepared mustard

ONION

    1 medium onion = 1 tablespoon onion powder

    1 small onion = 1 tablespoon dried minced onion

SELF-RISING FLOUR

    1 cup sifted self-rising flour = 1 cup sifted all-purpose flour plus

    1½ teaspoons baking powder and ½ teaspoon salt

SOUR CREAM

    1 cup sour cream = 1 cup plain yogurt or 1 cup cottage cheese pureed in a

    blender with 1 tablespoon lemon juice and ⅓ cup butter

UNSWEETENED BAKING CHOCOLATE

    1 ounce unsweetened baking chocolate = 3 tablespoons unsweetened cocoa

    plus 1 tablespoon butter or shortening

VANILLA BEAN

    ½ bean = 1 tablespoon vanilla extract

WHIPPING CREAM

    1 cup whipping cream, unwhipped = 2 cups whipped topping

WINE

    1 cup wine = 1 cup grape, cranberry, or apple juice

Weights and Measures Know-How

The Cheat Sheet

While Martha knows how to convert every kitchen measurement known to womankind, I find that I'm frequently in need of a little help. Please use this cheat sheet when you find you've forgotten how to convert tablespoons to teaspoons, pints to ounces, quarts to cups, and everything in between.

½ tablespoon = 1½ teaspoons

1 tablespoon = 3 teaspoons

¼ cup = 4 tablespoons

⅓ cup = 5 tablespoons + 1 teaspoon

½ cup = 8 tablespoons

½ pint = 1 cup (or 8 fluid ounces)

1 pint = 2 cups (or 16 fluid ounces)

1 quart = 4 cups (or 2 pints or 32 fluid ounces)

1 gallon = 16 cups (or 4 quarts)

1 pound = 16 ounces

1 peck = 8 quarts

1 bushel = 4 pecks

Index

BEVERAGES

BREADS

CANDIES

CONDIMENTS

DESSERTS

MAIN DISHES

Be sure to join us

next time in the kitchen with. . .

Mary & Martha's One-Dish Wonders

Coming in April 2006.

Available wherever books are sold.